TRICKS OF THE ANTIQUE TRADE

First published June 1975

SBN   0-902921-22-3

Published by Lyle Publications Glenmayne Galashiels Selkirkshire Scotland

TRICKS OF THE ANTIQUE TRADE

Tony Curtis
and Stuart Barton

LYLE PUBLICATIONS   **GLENMAYNE · GALASHIELS**

ACKNOWLEDGEMENTS

The publishers wish to acknowledge and thank the following for their kind help and assistance in the production of this book.

Shiela Porteous
Peter Knox
Norma Tweedie
John Martin
Anne Swanchett
Annette Hogg
King & Chasemore
Dowell's, Edinburgh
Bradley & Vaughan
Henry Spencer & Sons
Sotheby & Co
Wallis & Wallis
Heathershaws
Tweeddale Press

Printed and bound by Morrison & Gibb, Edinburgh, on paper supplied by Robert Hall & Co.

INTRODUCTION

One of the most popularly-voiced attributes of antique objects is the high degree of craftsmanship usually employed in their manufacture. Regardless of style, period or materials, this quality stands as a permanent reminder of skills almost forgotten and pride in workmanship almost unheard of among the producers of today's production line furniture.

It is largely this quality of good workmanship which has been responsible for the survival of so many objects of great age — that and the care which has been lavished upon them by generations of owners and servants who were prepared (or obliged) to devote a proper amount of time and effort to the proper upkeep of their household effects.

During the twentieth century, the industrial nations have tended to squander the material resources of the planet while setting a premium on the two resources which will last as long as man himself — time and effort. We have learned, falsely, that anything which will save time, any quick, easy method of doing things is by definition good. It is perhaps not surprising, therefore, that two of the most common causes of permanent damage to antiques seem to be the result of the very best intentions. Over-harsh cleaning methods on the one hand, and ill-informed attempts at repair on the other must, between them, be responsible for thousands of pounds worth of damage each year: damage which could have been prevented by proper employment of time and effort.

The cardinal rules when contemplating cleaning or repairing any object of value — Take your time. Find out the correct procedure before you begin and, unless you positively know your methods are perfectly safe, don't do it! The old adage, 'act in haste, repent at leisure', is as true now as ever it was.

Modern technology has produced much that is of great assistance to the skilled restorer, including new and powerful adhesives, incredibly durable finishes and a whole armoury of power tools. Used incorrectly or carelessly, however, any of these can do incalculable harm and may even place the 'repaired' object beyond redemption by even the most skilled of professional restorers.

Every procedure described in this book is a tried and tested method of cleaning, caring for or repairing antique objects. In many cases, safe temporary repairs have been suggested alongside (or instead of) more permanent repairs demanding a high degree of skill or specialised experience.

Tony Curtis

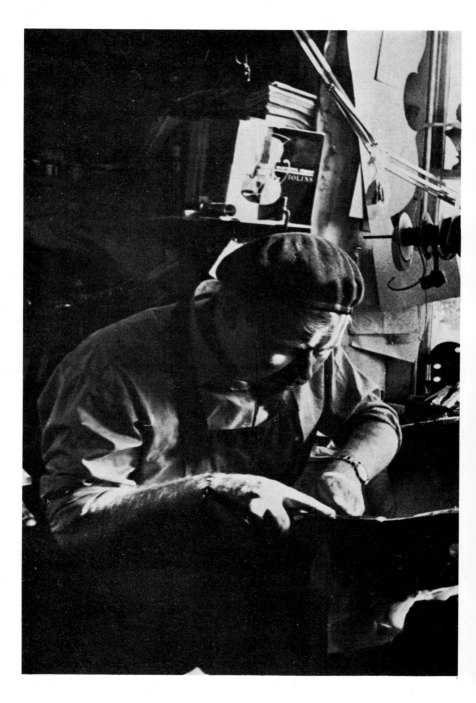

TRICKS OF THE ANTIQUE TRADE

The information contained in this book is listed under headings arranged alphabetically. These headings relate either to the problem concerned (e.g. Arms, Loose and Broken), the process, (e.g. Bleaching) the material, (e.g. Bronze) or the object (e.g. Chronometers). In this way, it is hoped, the reader will most easily be able to find the required information without having to plough through reams of type irrelevant to the particular problem on hand.

Wherever possible, the text describes at least two repair methods — one, a simple, makeshift method aimed more at disguising damage than repairing it, the other, an authentic technique whose proper application will result in a permanently effective repair. Equally important (if not more so) there are occasional references to commonly employed 'butchery' techniques which should be avoided at all costs. It cannot be stressed too strongly that faulty 'repairs' made with the wrong materials are worse than no repair at all — and not infrequently result in the complete ruination of a potentially beautiful or valuable object.

ABRASIVES

Although any number of abrasive materials are available in granule form, the most convenient to use are those with paper or cloth backing — emery paper, emery cloth, glasspaper etc.

Normally their use is part of the finishing process and it is usual to begin with a coarse grade, changing to finer grades as the task progresses.

Metals and glass require emery and carborundum, both of which are extremely hard, while wood is more normally treated with glasspaper (normally called sandpaper) or garnet paper. Steel wool is used on softer metals and wood.

Once a metal, glass or stone surface has been rendered smooth by the use of coarser abrasives it is frequently polished with mild abrasives including crocus powder, jeweller's rouge, whiting and talc (french chalk) applied dry or as a paste on a piece of chamois or soft cloth.

ACIDS

Expressed in the simplest of generalisations, acid atoms are those which carry a positive charge. When these are brought into contact with negatively charged atoms (alkali atoms carry a negative charge) there is a more or less violent reaction which results in a neutral substance — a salt. The violence of the reaction depends on the relative strengths of the acids and alkalis concerned.

Strong acids include sulphuric, nitric and hydrochloric acid. These are all extremely dangerous substances which should be treated at all times with the greatest of caution. Brought into contact with the skin, they will cause serious burns frequently followed by permanent scars.

Weaker acids include acetic, citric and oxalic acid. Although not as immediately dangerous as the stronger acids, these should, nevertheless, be treated with respect, particularly oxalic acid which is poisonous if taken internally.

When vinegar or lemon juice is mentioned in the text it is because these contain acetic and citric acid respectively in concentrations which are perfectly safe.

General rules for the storage and handling of acids are these.

1. Always keep acids in the containers in which the chemist supplied them, ensuring that they are clearly labelled and stored in a locked cupboard containing nothing else.
2. When diluting acids, **always** add acid to water, **never** water to acid.
3. In the event of accidental spillage on the skin or clothes, flood **immediately** with running water. To facilitate this, acids should only ever be used close to a water supply.
4. When you finish working with acids, always clear up meticulously, restoppering bottles and returning them to their cupboard. Dispose of all waste, washing containers and surfaces on which drops may have been spilled.

ALABASTER

Alabaster is a translucent stone which is sometimes mistaken for marble. It is generally softer than marble, however, and easier to work, and has been a popular sculptor's material at various times — notably during the eighteenth century when it was widely used in the manufacture of clocks and other ornamental pieces.

Usually white, the material can be yellow, brown or pink, often with streaks and blotches indicating impurities. It is a fine-grained stone and is usually given a high polish but, being soft, is easily scratched, bruised and broken. The softer varieties are porous and slightly soluble, to the extent that water alone may damage the high-gloss surface. For this reason, alabaster should never be washed but should be cleaned with a solvent such as petrol, alcohol or acetone applied sparingly on a soft cloth or fine brush.

Stubborn stains may yield to a weak ammonia solution applied sparingly. This will almost certainly damage the surface finish and should never be tried on pieces of value.

Broken pieces may be stuck with a polyvinyl acetate adhesive and should be held together under pressure while this sets. Where direct pressure cannot be easily applied, strips of sellotape may be used stuck across the join at right angles to it.

Where the surface of a piece of alabaster has become pitted, the finest grade of wet-or-dry paper can be used to rub it down. Final repolishing is best done with a small quantity of

19th century white marble nude contained within a pink and white alabaster shell. Although the marble figure could be washed quite safely, this could damage the alabaster.

good quality white wax polish. Bruises in the stone cannot be treated, but small chips can sometimes be disguised by rubbing in a little warm paraffin wax.

AMBER

The fossilized resin of primeval conifers, amber has long been prized in the East and elsewhere, often believed to be imbued with magical and regeneratory powers.

Cleaning should not be undertaken lightly, particularly where the piece is of value. Soap and water in moderation will remove most surface dirt, and the piece should be rinsed and thoroughly dried immediately after washing. Ingrained dirt will probably yield to a very careful application of acetone sparingly applied on a soft cloth. This can be extremely dangerous, however, since it can cause the amber to soften and even dissolve.

Epoxy resin adhesives are recommended for repairs to amber.

ARCHAEOLOGICAL SPECIMENS

Specimens of archaeological interest can turn up at any time and the first reaction of most people finding a curious object while digging the garden is to get it cleaned up so that they can have a good look at it.

Fossils are by far the most frequent finds and these, being stone, can usually be cleaned up quite safely under the tap but, if you wish to learn anything about your find, the best course is to put it, uncleaned, into a polythene bag and take it to your local museum where they may often discover clues to its age in the earth in which it was found.

Pottery fragments, too, are usually pretty robust and will rarely be harmed by washing but, again, the staff of your museum will be happy to advise on the best treatment and, perhaps, be able to tell you something of the age and uses to which the pot was put. If you find enough fragments which appear to have come from the same pot, and if you have a great deal of patience, these may be carefully glued together and any gaps filled with plaster of paris.

Metal objects, on the other hand, should always be taken to the museum just as they are. Some, particularly iron objects may be so corroded that any but the most skilled attention will result in their total destruction, and others, of bronze, may be affected by Bronze Disease and in need of treatment.

Never use abrasives on any archaeological specimens — even fine metal polish can cause irreparable harm — and, when washing them, use only cold or warm water, soap and a soft brush, leaving them to dry without heat.

A useful preservative for most objects is polyvinyl acetate, which may be bought in powder form from some chemists, and this should be applied only after you are certain that any decomposing process has been properly checked (fossils and pottery are unlikely to need protective coatings of any kind).

Never glue specimens onto a backing material for display — you will almost certainly wish to move them sooner or

later and removal of the glue can rarely be achieved without damaging the object in some way. If it is essential that specimens be secured for display, use fine thread or pins to hold them in place.

A useful book for those who wish to go deeper into the subject is *Conservation in Field Archaeology*, by Elizabeth A. Downer and published by Methuen.

ARMS LOOSE AND BROKEN

When the arm of a chair is loose or broken there is only one way to set about repairing it and that is to remove it completely from the rest of the frame.

1. With a chisel, remove all traces of old glue, taking great care not to remove any wood from either mortices or tenons since this will cause the joints to be loose when they are re-glued.

2. If the arm is broken cleanly it may be possible to simply glue the pieces together but a better way would be to insert a dowel. To do this, carefully mark the broken pieces so that when they have been drilled, the holes will exactly match. The hole should be just large enough to take the dowel without forcing but the fit should be tight. When using ready made dowel rod, check the size against that of your drill because there are always slight variations between the nominal and actual sizes of prepared timber of all kinds.

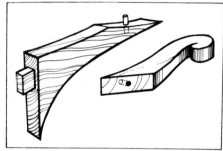

3. Apply plenty of glue and make sure that it gets right into the holes. Insert the dowel and cramp the pieces together, wiping off the squeezed-out glue before it sets.

Leave the arm at least overnight before releasing the pressure and fixing it back on the chair.

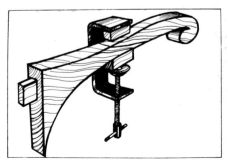

4. When the arm is reglued to the chair, pressure must again be applied while the glue is setting.

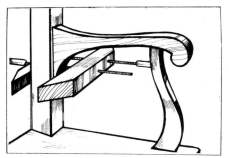

Never use nails, metal plates or angle-pieces to repair furniture: they may seem to offer the simplest means at the time but they are never as satisfactory in the long run as properly glued joints, and their use will always detract from the value of the piece.

Screws may sometimes be safely used, but generally only in conjunction with a glued join, — and their heads must always be concealed. In a case such as this — the repair of a chair arm — the screw would normally be well countersunk and a round plug of wood used to conceal its location.

If the tenon joint is broken:

1. Saw off the broken piece.

Carefully clean all old glue from the mortice.

2. Using a wood as nearly as possible matching the original timber, cut a plug which will exactly fill the mortice hole and glue it in.

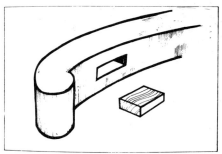

3. Drill holes for a dowel (or two, if the joint is large) in both pieces to be rejoined.

Apply plenty of glue and continue as from 4 above.

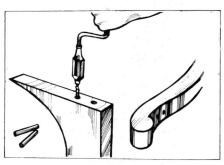

As an alternative to the dowel method, a broken tenon may be repaired by making what is, in effect, a new tenon.

1. Clean out the mortice as before, removing all broken or papery wood from the hole but keeping it rectangular.

Cut a piece of wood to fit the mortice

but make its length about twice the depth of the mortice hole.

2. After sawing the broken tenon off cleanly, cut a mortice hole in the arm to accept your new tenon. A dowel can be inserted for extra strength.

3. The whole joint can be glued, assembled and cramped in one go or, if preferred, the tenon can be glued into the mortice first and then into its slot later.

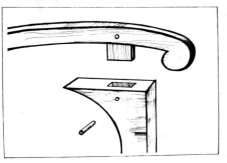

When an arm is broken, but not cleanly, the only alternatives are to replace the entire arm or, at least, a large part of it.

When the chair is in use, it is normally advisable to replace the arm in its entirety but, in cases where the chair is more of a display piece, it might be better to effect a repair which should be carried out as follows.

1. Cut the arm back to the sound wood.

   Matching grain and colour as closely as possible, cut a new section to replace the discarded part.

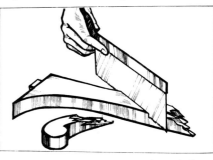

2. The splice should be made as below, this being much stronger than a splice which runs parallel to the sides of the wood.

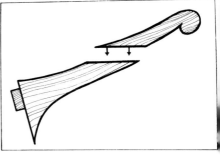

3. Glue and cramp the splice into position.

   Recut any joints in the new wood and continue as above.

ASTRAGAL GLAZING

Early 19th century Astragal glazed bookcase in need of repair.

Cutting glass is one of those jobs which experts make look easy and beginners always mess up — largely as a result of nervousness.

Always buy an expensive cutter; it will more than save its price in a very short time.

Always work on a perfectly flat surface — a dining table protected by a couple of sheets of newspaper is usually recommended.

The problem with cutting glass for astragal glazing lies mainly in the shapes to be cut — they are rarely, if ever, rectangles — but there are three relatively simple methods of ensuring that the pieces of glass you cut will be of the right shape and size to replace those that are missing.

If several panes are broken in the same door:

1. Remove the door and lay it face down on a flat table (you will probably have to remove the door

furniture to allow it to lie flat). Using a reasonably sized sheet of glass, lay it over the first space to be filled so that one of its edges is properly aligned with the rebated beading and will not have to be cut.

With your eye directly above the work, lay a straight edge about $\frac{1}{8}$ of an inch nearer the centre of the panel than the first cut required (this is because your cutter point lies about that distance away from the side of the tool).

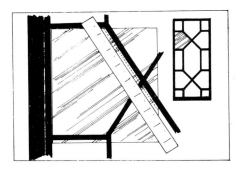

2. Working toward yourself, score the glass from the furthest edge and continue right across the sheet. Do not break away the waste glass yet.

Without moving the glass, reposition your straight edge for the next cut and score the opposite edge of the pane in the same way.

The third cut should be made to join the score marks made by the previous two. Never use your cutter to cross score marks already in the glass as this is extremely liable to damage its point.

Your sheet of glass could now look something like this.

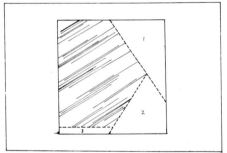

3. Once all the score marks are made, the glass can be removed from the door and the waste broken away in the same order that the cuts were made (i.e. only attempt to break away pieces which have been scored from edge to edge of the remaining glass).

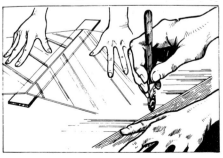

If only one or two panes are missing from the same door:

Either cut a paper template to fit the space and use this under the glass, proceeding as above, or coat one surface of the glass with metal polish and, once this is dry, draw with a fine point the shape you wish to cut and carry on in the usual way.

BAMBOO FURNITURE

The hollow nature of bamboo is such that furniture made of it tends to be rather creaky and insecure. It also rules out all the more usual methods of repair.

The usual damage sustained by bamboo is splitting and splintering; the only way of repairing it entails the insertion of suitably diametered dowel rod.

Generally, however, the splintering is confined to the lower reaches of chair and table legs — the parts that receive the most wear. If the bamboo is too badly damaged, the only thing to do is to remove the entire section (sawing through just below the first undamaged ring) and either replace it with new bamboo or convince yourself that you prefer low-level furniture anyway.

Replacement is achieved by dowelling sections together — which is not always as simple as it might sound.

1. Find a piece of bamboo the same diameter as the piece to be replaced. If its colour matches nicely so much the better but this can be attended to later.

Saw one or more complete sections (depending on the length you need) from the new bamboo.

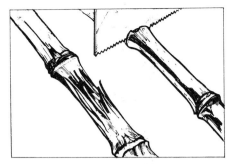

4. Apply plenty of glue to your dowel and to the inside of one section of bamboo and push the dowel halfway into the glued tube.

When the glue has set, repeat the process with the other bamboo section and leave it for at least twelve hours before returning the article to use.

2. Drill through the solid section of the rings to be joined and, with a chisel or round file, extend the diameter of the hole until it is the same as that of the hollow bamboo beyond it.

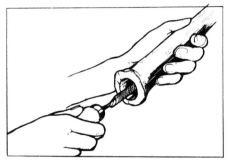

5. If necessary, colour the new section of wood with dyes to match the rest of the object.

If, for any reason, replacement of a section is impossible, splintered bamboo may be repaired by inserting a dowel rod in the same manner as described above and, using Araldite or other epoxy resin, sticking the splintered parts down onto the dowel. Cotton or other fine thread can be used to bind the splinters down while the adhesive sets, and this can be removed when the resin has 'gone off' but before it has fully hardened. Any missing pieces can be built up with Araldite or Plastic Padding and coloured to match the surrounding wood.

As regards finishing, bamboo should never be sanded because it has a smooth hard outer surface which is quite different in colour and appearance from the cane beneath.

Wax polish or a polyurethane lacquer are generally recommended finishes for all articles of bamboo.

3. Since you are unlikely to be lucky enough to find a piece of dowel which exactly fits into the bamboo tubes, pare down a larger piece so that it makes a tight fit for both tubes — the farther it extends into the tubes the better.

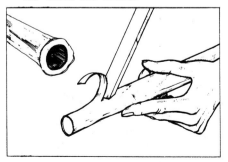

BAROMETERS

Barometers are instruments used to predict changes in the weather by registering alterations in atmospheric pressure.

The simplest, and earliest, barometers register atmospheric pressure by means of a long glass tube containing mercury. The upper end of the tube is always sealed. The lower end may have a U-bend and terminate in an open, bulb-shaped cistern, or it may simply stand in a reservoir (often made of boxwood) containing mercury. In banjo, or wheel, barometers, the open lower end of the tube makes a U-turn, and a glass weight resting on top of the mercury is connected via a pulley to the pointer which registers changes on a round dial.

Under no circumstances should the mercury be removed from the tube or the tube from the barometer

A late 18th century banjo barometer in a Sheraton-style case.

case, since the result is certain to be nothing better than an inaccurate barometer (even assuming you manage to get all the mercury back into the tube).

In some cases a sticking pointer on a mercury barometer of the banjo type is caused by nothing more serious than dirt. What usually occurs is that small pieces of sticky or gritty dust insinuate themselves between the wall of the tube and the glass weights mentioned above.

If this is suspected prop the instrument, face down, at an angle of forty five degrees or more to the horizontal. Ensure, above all, that the barometer cannot slip — the slightest accident will cause the mercury to flow out of the open end of the tube.

Carefully withdraw one glass weight from its tube and wipe it with a clean rag soaked in lighter fuel to

A pediment barometer. The mercury column should not be removed.

remove all greasy dirt. Replace the weight and repeat the process with the other one.

If the weights are missing, under no circumstances replace them with metal weights — these will almost certainly become amalgamated with the mercury which will itself lose its peculiar properties.

Remember, too, that mercury is a poisonous and extremely dangerous substance.

Generally, however, it will be the wooden case which is in most need of care and attention — perhaps to the extent where repolishing is felt to be called for.

This can be a tricky business since, as already mentioned, the mercury tube should not be removed from the instrument, and it is obviously impossible to do a full-scale stripping and repolishing job with the tube in place — remember, a mercury barometer must never be laid flat. All that can be done, therefore, is a patch-up job, tinting and filling scratches to match as nearly as possible the surrounding finish.

Broken thermometers can, of course, be replaced though care should be exercised when choosing replacements to ensure that they are of the right size and scale.

Brass flanges and other decorative features of the same metal can be cleaned and re-lacquered. Dial faces and scales, if of enamel, can be treated in the same manner as clock faces. Parchment scales are best left unrestored.

Later barometers are usually of the 'aneroid' type, which operate by means of one or more partially-evacuated metal drums whose faces move with changes in atmospheric pressure. As with barometers of the mercury type, little or nothing can be done to repair the actual mechanisms of these at home.

A typical Victorian aneroid barometer.

A development of the aneroid barometer is the barograph. Instead of registering atmospheric pressure on a dial which also predicts the weather, the barograph is fitted with a pen which records atmospheric pressures on a chart fixed to the outside of a revolving drum.

Owing to their delicacy and precision, barographs should not be tampered with more than is absolutely necessary. Cleaning may be carried out with care, dust and grease being removed with a soft brush, perhaps moistened with a little lighter fuel. Lubrication should be minimal.

Any more extensive repairs to the mechanism should be entrusted to a professional.

A barograph with paper chart in position.

BASKETWORK

Basketwork is simply wickerwork by another name. That is, it is made of woven osiers (willow twigs) as opposed to one of the various canes used in canework.

One disadvantage of basketwork is that the osiers tend to become brittle with age, often breaking away in short sections and leaving unsightly gaps. In some cases, these broken pieces can be simply glued back into place with a contact or woodworking adhesive — for instance, where the basketwork is woven round a stone jar.

Where breakages reduce the structural strength of the piece, however, there is really no alternative to replacing the missing pieces and although willow is more generally employed — the twigs being fairly long and flexible — any other suitable wood can be used, and hazel is particularly good. The twigs are best gathered in the early summer, when they are at their most flexible, and are easiest to use while they are still green. A soak in a bath of hot water will be found to increase flexibility.

Remove all broken and loose sections of twig from the piece being repaired and simply re-weave with new wood. A largish pair of pliers will be useful for gripping and bending the twigs. Ends are simply tucked away out of sight.

When the new wood has dried out — a few weeks indoors will usually be long enough for this — the whole piece can be given a rub over with liquid wax or treated with a matt polyurethane varnish.

BEADWORK

Beadwork is best cleaned by washing it carefully in warm, soapy water after which it should immediately be dried in a warm atmosphere because some of the beads may tend to rust if left wet for too long.

Missing beads can be replaced with a needle and thread as a rule, though, sometimes, the holes in smaller beads will be found to be too small to admit the passage of even the finest needle. When this is the case, there are three alternatives.

When only one or two small beads are involved among several others which allow the use of a needle, the obvious way is to remove the needle and thread a bead onto the cotton, rethreading the needle to make the stitch.

Fine nylon thread (single filament, like fine fishing line) can sometimes be used without a needle.

For quick, temporary repairs, or when the beadwork is mounted behind glass (as in a fire screen) individual beads can be glued into place using Copydex or other rubber based adhesive applied in spots onto the cloth backing. This should be done only *after* the work has been washed and thoroughly dried.

BENTWOOD

A 19th century bentwood rocker with cane back. The solid seat was put in place of a damaged cane seat.

This is extremely difficult to repair effectively and the reason lies in the way furniture is made by this method. As the name implies, the wood is bent into shape and, although it is steamed before being formed into curves, it retains some resilience and tends to split rather badly once it is damaged.

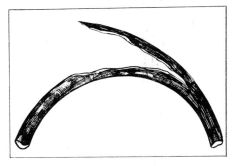

Frankly, once dirt and grease has got into the split, there is little chance of effecting a satisfactory repair, though a thorough wash with a spirit-based cleanser might help.

Having cleaned the raw, split wood, force plenty of glue (a goose feather is a useful aid here) as far as possible into the split and, starting at the closed end, apply cramps every couple of inches along the section to be repaired. Leave

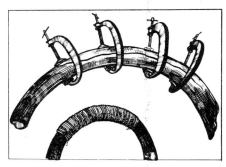

for at least eight hours before releasing the pressure, bearing in mind that, if it springs apart again, you will be unable to clean the wood effectively for a second attempt.

Fortunately, bentwood furniture is cheap enough to be considered more or less disposable and, in most cases, repairs might be felt to be more expensive than they are worth.

BLEACHING

Bleaching of wood is often desirable for a variety of reasons; it might be that the natural colour of the wood is darker than required or that it has been previously stained to resemble a different kind of timber. Some stripping preparations, too, cause a darkening of the wood which may be acceptable or may need to be bleached.

Then there are the blotches and streaks caused accidentally — usually by bad storage or failure to wipe split liquids from surfaces, and there are the spots and stains which disfigure prints, textiles and ceramics. Most, if not all of these, can be treated to reduce the unwanted colour at least to the point where its presence is unnoticeable.

To bleach raw wood

Probably the best method of bleaching raw wood is to treat it with common or garden household bleach; Parazone, Brobat and Domestos are three of the better known types and, despite manufacturers' advertising claims, all are equally effective. Whichever brand is chosen, it should be used diluted at first and only applied at full strength as a last resort to obtain the absolute maximum effect. Once the bleaching process is completed and the colour of the wood reduced to the required level, the wood should be thoroughly flooded with fresh water to remove all traces of bleach, bearing in mind that a certain amount will have been absorbed into the wood and, if not washed away, will tend to have an adverse effect on subsequent finishes applied to the article.

Wood treated in this way should have the surface moisture wiped off with a cloth and should then be left to dry out slowly and naturally without heat. Attempts at quick drying are liable to cause warping and even splitting of the wood, particularly when it has been wet for some time and moisture has soaked deeply. Needless to say, efforts should be made to reduce to a minimum the amount of soaking to which glued joints are subjected during the bleaching and washing processes — many of the older, pre-resin glues are water soluble.

To remove blotches, streaks, spots and stains

The commonest unsightly stains on furniture are caused by spilled liquids such as ink, water and alcohol, and by cigarette burns. When these are not sufficiently extensive to justify stripping the article and starting from scratch, they can often be treated individually, provided care is exercised.

Ink will usually be found to yield to an application of weak, say five percent, solution of nitric acid or to a combination of vinegar and Milton (Milton is disinfectant sold for sterilizing baby feeding bottles and teats). Dab on a little vinegar and add a little Milton, repeating as necessary, and finish by washing in clean water before drying and repolishing.

Water stains on table tops are usually black and streaky, and are caused by spilled water penetrating the polish and soaking into the wood beneath. These should be treated with a saturated

solution of oxalic acid, which can be brushed carefully onto the stained area and washed off with water once the bleaching effect has reached the desired level. If left, oxalic acid will continue to bleach wood until it is lighter than it originally was — that is, it will remove the natural colour from the wood — necessitating the bleached area being re-stained to blend with the surrounding colour.

Oxalic acid can be bought in crystal form from decorators' suppliers and, to make a saturated solution, put about a quarter to half a pound into a pint bottle and add warm water. Some crystals will not dissolve and this is a sign that the solution is saturated. As the mixture is used, the bottle can be kept topped up with water until all crystals have dissolved — a sign that more are needed.

Oxalic acid is not a particularly harmful chemical but it stings cuts and scratches.

White water marks are caused by the slow evaporation of the liquid and can usually be removed from polished wood by rubbing with metal polish. If the mark has penetrated deeply it might be necessary to use the finest grade of steel wool (ooo grade) moistened with oil. This wears down the layer of polish on the wood and, if continued too far, will remove it entirely — in which case the area will have to be repolished. If the stain has penetrated this deeply, however, it is likely to be accompanied by the black mark mentioned above.

Alcohol stains are a problem owing to the fact that the alcohol dissolves french polish and penetrates freely to the wood beneath.

The first measure is to take a clean, lint free cloth and moisten it with a little linseed oil. Using this, stroke the mark lightly with meths and try to blend the polish over the mark.

If this method is ineffective, try ooo grade wire wool or flour paper and remove the polish entirely from the affected area, building up again with fresh french polish (applied, like stain, with the grain).

Cigarette burns

Cigarette burns are probably the worst marks of all because they not only discolour the wood, they also frequently char it to the extent that a dent is left.

First of all, sand the mark carefully with a fine gauge paper to remove only the loose charred wood and try treating it with neat household bleach. If this fails — and it very often does — the only thing to do is to make a feature of the burn.

Strip the polish back along the grain for a distance of a few inches and then, using a fine paint brush and a dark wood stain paint a tapering streak on the wood to resemble the kind of dark figuring found naturally. If, as is usually the case, the cigarette burn is situated on the edge of the surface, carry the stain down to a reasonable depth over the edge if necessary. If the burn is small, it can sometimes be disguised to resemble a tiny knot in the wood. When the stain has dried, repolish the area, blending the new and old polish until you cannot see the join.

Porcelain

Cracks in porcelain can very often be treated with household bleach in order to reduce their colour. A fairly weak solution should be used and this can be applied by soaking a rag or piece of cotton wool and applying this along the length of the crack for a day or two, adding more solution to the rag as it dries out. Wash the piece thoroughly in clean water after treatment is complete.

Owing to the porous nature of much English porcelain, this frequently fails to respond to treatment — Chinese and European porcelains, being less porous, are more likely to benefit.

Paper

Prints, etchings and watercolours frequently fall prey to rust spots and fox marks. Watercolours present their own problems because of the impermanent nature of the paint. These are best left to experts.

Prints, drawings, etchings and so on can have their fox marks removed by immersing them first in a solution of one ounce of chloride of lime dissolved in a gallon of distilled water and then in four fluid ounces of hydrochloric acid mixed with one gallon of distilled water.

Photographic suppliers sell plastic or enamel dishes which are excellent for this purpose but, naturally, great care must be exercised when handling the wet paper. A sheet of glass is useful in this respect. Placed in the bottom of the dish, the print can be laid above it and both lifted from the solutions together, the glass providing an excellent support for the wet paper.

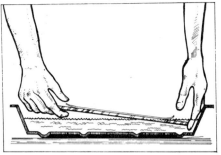

Chlorine gas makes an excellent, if deadly, bleach for prints but, naturally, its use demands a great deal of care and an airtight box in which the print can be placed while it is subjected to the action of the gas. A glass lid to the box enables the bleaching process to be observed.

Having made a suitably sized box (or converted an old drawer), drill a hole in one side and fix into this a piece of glass or rigid plastic tubing, sealing it with putty or other, similar, compound.

The gas is made in a large glass jar (gallon wine bottle) with a rubber bung through which passes another piece of tubing the same diameter as that used for the box. Rubber or flexible plastic tubing is used to lead the gas from jar to box.

Damp the print to be bleached with water and lay it on a sheet of

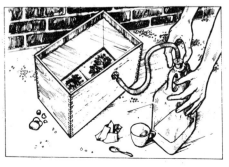

glass in the bottom of your gas chamber. Close the lid. Check that the flexible tube is properly connected to box and jar stopper.

Into the jar, put two ounces of chloride of lime (bleaching powder) and add a cupful of accumulator acid. Push the bung tightly in.

Really, this process is best carried out in the open air but, if that is not convenient, a well ventilated room with all doors and windows open will be quite safe since the amount of gas generated using the above quantities of chemical is insufficient to constitute a serious risk to health provided reasonable care is taken.

Once the print is sufficiently bleached, simply open the lid of the box and allow the gas to disperse in the air, taking care not to inhale it. Never carry out this process in a room with pets as they are likely to be far more susceptible to small concentrations of chlorine gas than humans.

BONE

Bone is softer and less durable than ivory and, therefore, more likely to be found in poor condition.

Articles which are badly cracked should be impregnated with paraffin wax which will help to preserve them. To do this, first warm the article thoroughly and then immerse it in a bath of melted wax for a few minutes, wiping off the surplus wax while it is still runny.

Cleaning is best carried out with a paste of whiting and twenty volume hydrogen peroxide. Spread the paste over the object to be cleaned and stand it in the sun to dry. Wash it off carefully with swabs of cotton wool moistened with a little water and dry the piece thoroughly with a soft cloth. Repeat the process if necessary and finish off by applying a little almond oil.

Broken pieces should be stuck back on with clear acetate glue before immersion in wax but replacement parts are best added afterward so that the final colour of the piece can be matched.

BONE INLAY

Bone inlay that has become loose may be cleaned of all old adhesive and glued back into place. Where the piece is missing, a new piece can often be cut from a dry beef bone and filed to size with needle files, or white wax can be dripped into the hole and polished level with the surrounding surface. It may be necessary to add a small quantity of brown or yellow to the white wax to ensure a good colour match with the original bone.

Careful applications of pale shoe polish will prove an effective colourant which can be reduced as necessary by polishing with metal polish.

BOOKS

If books are to be properly preserved they must be handled regularly and not left to moulder in a glass fronted bookcase. They need air and, if leather bound, they need a certain amount of grease to keep the leather supple.

Too much or too little humidity will speed books' deterioration, as will too much heat or sunshine, and the problem is that the damage is usually done before any outward signs appear.

Leather bindings are particularly unsightly once they have started to deteriorate visibly. No amount of polishing will restore them to their original state, so the only alternatives are to patch or replace them.

If the damage is confined to a relatively small area, it will probably be

worthwhile to patch it and this is not too difficult provided it is done with care.

First, cut away the area of leather to be replaced, carefully cleaning away all dirt and old adhesive from the cardboard cover and lifting the edges of the surrounding leather. If possible, pare the underside down to make it taper away to nothing. Having cut your patch from a piece of suitable thickness and colour, pare the edges of this (lay it face down and rub the back with sandpaper until the edges just begin to fray).

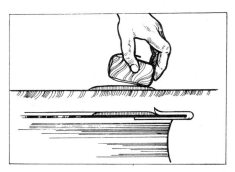

Apply glue to the cardboard book cover, ensuring that it is spread evenly and thinly, and extend it under the raised edges, carefully positioning your patch so that the old leather overlaps the new. Wipe away all traces of glue which ooze out onto the patched area and leave it to dry under pressure before attempting to blend away any variations in colour.

Colour can usually be matched fairly easily with carefully applied water paints, building up the colour with several coats where necessary. A final rub over with a proprietary leather dressing such as Sheerwax should hold the colour fast.

If the book cover is so badly damaged as to need replacing, it can be done at home but valuable books should be sent to a professional bookbinder whose services are costly but worthwhile.

A new cover can be made and fitted fairly easily to any book whose pages have not become unstitched.

1. Cut two equal sized pieces of stiff card about ¼ inch larger than the pages. Cut, too, a piece of thin card for the spine.
2. Cut a strip of linen to extend along the full length of the stitched end of the pages and about one inch wider than the thickness of the pages. Glue this along the spine of the book.
3. Lay your leather out flat and glue onto the reverse side the three pieces of card which will form the covers and spine of the book. These should be positioned so that there is a gap of three sixteenths of an inch between them. Trim the leather as shown.
Fold over the edges of the leather; top and bottom first, then sides. Glue them firmly.

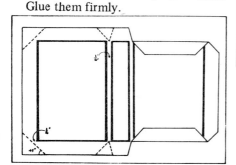

4. Allow a few hours for all the glue to dry thoroughly.
5. Now spread a film of glue about three quarters of an inch wide down the inside of each cardboard cover along the edge nearest the spine.
6. Holding the pages of the book upright, stand them in the spine and fix the loose edges of linen to the covers.

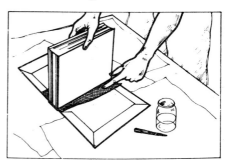

7. Cut two sheets of strong white or coloured paper for the end papers. These should be the same size as the book when it is laid open — that is, twice the size of a single page.
8. Glue the end papers to covers.

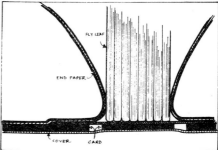

9. Run a narrow strip of glue (about $\frac{1}{8}$ inch) along the spine edge of the outside pages of the book (fly leaves) and glue the end papers to these.

Titles can be written carefully onto the leather binding in indian ink or, for the more ambitious, they can be tooled using the tooling wheels which may be bought at any good art and crafts shop.

Leather bindings are sometimes found to be crumbling with age. These may respond to treatment with a mixture of three parts castor oil or two parts alcohol. This should be applied fairly liberally but with care not to allow it to spread to the pages. After it has soaked in (allow at least a day) give a coat of pure castor oil and polish gently.

If all that is wrong is that the leather is dirty, test it for colour fastness with a wet paintbrush in a spot which will not show. Assuming that the colour does not run, moisten a wad of cotton wool with warm water and soap (not detergent), squeeze it almost dry and wipe the book carefully. Never rub too hard; remember that the leather is old and paper thin.

Stains may be found to respond to a gentle wipe with cotton wool moistened with lighter fuel.

Shoe dyes and polishes may be applied very lightly to restore colour or to tone down around ugly stains that will not respond to cleaning treatments.

Mould should be treated with a proprietary fungicide.

If the leather has become hard and inflexible, a liberal dose of saddle soap can do nothing but good. Apply this with a damp sponge or soft paintbrush and work it well in.

A particularly good treatment for leather is known in the trade as British Museum Leather Dressing:

Shred half an ounce of beeswax into eleven ounces of hexane (this is a highly inflammable liquid and should not be exposed to heat). Stir or shake until the beeswax is completely dissolved. Stir in seven ounces of anhydrous lanolin

followed by one ounce of cedar wood oil. This mixture should be shaken well before use and applied with a soft cloth to leather binding, taking care not to allow it to spread onto the pages of the book.

Having dealt with bindings, attention can now be turned to the pages.

General dirt and grime can usually be removed with breadcrumbs or a clean finger dipped in potato flour. More stubborn marks can be rubbed gently with the softest of artists' erasers.

To remove grease spots from the pages, place a sheet of grease proof paper under the page being treated and moisten the spots with a fine brush dipped in white spirit or ether.

Fox marks can often be reduced or removed by means of a mixture of equal quantities of hydrogen peroxide and methylated spirits. This should be applied to individual marks with a paint brush. Several applications may be necessary and each should be left for a minute or so and then blotted dry before the next is applied. A final rinse of distilled water should always follow this treatment (tap water contains all kinds of things liable to do damage to the paper in the course of time and should be avoided).

Silverfish and other insects — even bookworms — can cause considerable damage, and any books which show signs of being used as housing or food supplies by insects should be shut overnight in an airtight case with a quantity of strong disinfectant (ammonia can be used for this).

Where insects have bored holes through the pages of a book, an amount of repair work will be necessary. Paper filler can be made in several ways:

Scrape a piece of paper with a scalpel or razor blade to produce a quantity of fluff. This can be mixed with flour paste.

Chew a piece of paper until it is completely pulpy.

For larger quantities, boil some paper with a little gelatine until it reaches the consistency of smooth porridge.

To fill holes (even quite large ones) with any of these preparations, lay a sheet of polythene under the page being treated and press the filler in firmly with the back of a spoon

or other smooth, hard object. All affected pages can be treated in one session so long as each repair is isolated from adjacent pages by a piece of polythene.

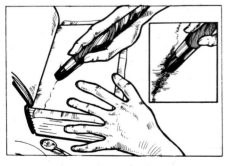

Tears can be repaired if a little time and trouble is taken:

Lay a sheet of glass under the page to be repaired (making sure that the edge of the glass is not doing any damage to the page beneath by binding it with adhesive tape).

With finger, or paintbrush, dipped in distilled water, wet the edges of the tear thoroughly and coax the fibres of the paper together, applying pressure to encourage them to interlock. Work in a small quantity of flour paste to ensure adhesion and press the join with the back of a spoon. Isolate the page between sheets of polythene and close the book, leaving it overnight to dry.

When the join has dried out thoroughly, lettering can be carefully touched up with indian ink. A very fine paint brush makes a better job of this than a pen.

Creases are often so bad that they can never be completely obliterated. Great improvements to the appearance of creased pages can, however, be made.

The damaged page should be damped thoroughly, isolated between sheets of clean paper and ironed with a moderately hot iron. **Do not use polythene to isolate the pages – it could melt.**

The appearance of many books is marred by grimy page edges. To clean these, the book must first be held tightly closed in a clamp of some kind which will allow no movement of the pages during treatment. Wipe the page edges with a piece of cotton wool and, when all loose dust has been removed, wipe them again with another piece of cotton wool moistened with ether. If the pages were gilded and this has become worn it can be brightened up considerably by means of a gold paste which can be bought from good art suppliers.

Badly worn pages can be rubbed down with very fine sandpaper (flour paper) and then treated with gilding paste.

BOXWOOD

Boxwood is a very hard, pale yellow wood, having a fine, close grain and very little figuring. For this reason it was widely used in turnery, for veneers, and as a material for making tools and tool handles. Nowadays it is quite difficult to obtain as a raw material and is consequently rather expensive.

Objects made of boxwood tend to darken with age to an attractive honey-colour, though sometimes accumulations of dirt and grease quite spoil the effect. Initial cleaning can be carried out with a minimal amount of soap and water (wiped or brushed on and carefully dried — never by immersion). Any solvent can be safely tried for the removal of stains and, where these fail, any of the bleaching methods described under the 'Bleaching' heading may be employed.

Wax polish is the best finish for objects made of boxwood.

BOXWOOD STRING INLAY

If the boxwood string inlay has come loose from a piece of furniture but is not completely detached, it should be removed before any attempt is made at sticking it back into place.

Try lifting out in its entirety but don't worry if it breaks off. Clean out the groove carefully, making sure that no wood is removed in the process. A fine, instrument maker's screwdriver is quite useful for this, being hard and sharp enough to do the job thoroughly and thin enough to fit into the groove easily.

Gently clean the glue from the inlay strip, again taking care not to remove any wood.

Lay fresh glue into the groove and press the inlay strip firmly into place,
wiping away all excess glue as it squeezes out.

When the piece of inlay is missing, there are two alternatives: Either cut a fresh strip of inlay or simply fill the groove with wax of the right colour.

Although it would be preferable to use proper boxwood to replace the missing inlay, a quite adequate substitute can be made from any light coloured veneer. The simplest of all to obtain is birch, which is the face veneer of most

good quality plywood. Using a metal straightedge and a single sided razor blade or scalpel, simply cut through the top two layers of the plywood and lift these carefully by cutting in through the edge of the sheet.

By taking two layers of veneer you are sure to have a strip which is slightly thicker than you need. Sand the reverse side of the strip to reduce its depth and glue this into place as described above.

This can be dyed to the right colour when it is in place, bearing in mind that the wet colour is not going to be the same as the finished result.

Some workers prefer to dye and polish their pieces of replacement inlay before fixing them. This ensures that no colouring errors can occur after the piece has been glued down and, although rather fiddly, is to be recommended as the best method for those who have not gained experience in judging colour changes which occur during polishing. Whichever way the job is done, try out colouring methods on a piece of waste veneer first.

BRASS

Brass, being an alloy of copper and zinc, generally may be treated in much the same way as copper. It is, however, a harder metal and less susceptible to scratching, so really dirty articles may sometimes be cautiously cleaned with fine wire wool — but only as a last resort. Chased and embossed articles will often demand prolonged attention with a stiff toothbrush moistened first with a solution of lemon juice and salt, finally with a proprietary metal polish.

Brass handles should always be removed from furniture before drastic cleaning methods are begun — though for routine cleaning, woodwork may be protected by sticky tape or a piece of card held against the edge of the metal.

Repairs to brass may be made with solder or epoxy resin adhesives.

BRASS INLAY

Loose or missing pieces of brass inlay may be either replaced or faked.

The replacement of brass in furniture involves the same procedure as the replacement of ordinary wood inlays — thorough cleaning of surfaces to be joined followed by a regluing job using a suitable adhesive. Brass presents one small problem of its own, however, in its tendency to develop a springiness which sometimes causes trouble during gluing. This is best combated by bending the brass slightly so that the middle of

A 19th century French brass inlaid card table.   Missing pieces of intricately-shaped brass can be simulated with coloured wax.

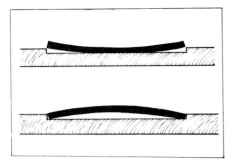

the piece bows upward to ensure that the ends or edges of the piece adhere properly to the wood beneath. As with all other gluing jobs, pressure must be applied while the adhesive sets.

Araldite is the adhesive to be recommended and, to ensure a firm hold, abrade the back of the piece of brass with emery paper and make sure that it is grease free by cleaning thoroughly with a spirit before applying the adhesive.

Where the piece of brass is too badly damaged to be replaced or is missing, yellow wax can be rubbed into the space and, when polished, this will pass all but the closest inspection.

BRONZE

The first and foremost rule' when dealing with bronze is never to use abrasives. Warm, soapy water should be used to remove dirt and care should be taken not to remove the patina along with it. The patina represents a considerable proportion of the value of a piece and can be destroyed in no time through over harsh cleaning methods.

Bronze figures and objects to be cleaned are best soaked for a while in warm, soapy water before being gently wiped or brushed with a soft nylon washing up brush. The harshest cleaning device that should ever be used (and then only in extreme cases of encrustation) is a brass wire brush — NEVER use a steel wire brush; apart from the damage this will do to the patina, it will ruin the actual surface of the bronze, covering it with fine scratches which are almost ineradicable. A weak (about 10%) solution of acetic acid may also be used in the removal of heavy encrustations.

The subject of bronze patination is one to which many experts have devoted a great deal of time. The colour of a patina will vary with the age of the piece, the atmospheric conditions to which it has been subjected and to the proportions of different metals used in its making. Generally, however, brown and green patinations are seen and these can be induced in a number of ways. One method of creating a brown patina is to heat the piece carefully and brush it with graphite. Another is to mix a solution of one part water to three of ammonium chloride and three of copper acetate. This is then boiled and the bronze placed in it. The longer the bronze is boiled in this solution, the darker the colour will be.

Green patination can be achieved by first applying to the bronze a weak solution of copper nitrate and salt. After about a week, apply a solution consisting of one hundred parts weak acetic acid (mix two parts of vinegar to one of water as a workable substitute) to five parts of ammonium chloride and one of oxalic acid. Once again the bronze should be left for about a week, though this solution may be re-applied as it dries out. Finally, wash the bronze in distilled water and allow to dry.

Apart from these chemical methods, which reasonably approximate the true patina of aged bronze, an appearance of patination can be achieved by the judicious use of renovating shoe polish — a little experimentation will determine the correct colours to be used. Dark tan, light tan, oxblood and green are the colours to use and these should be blended until the desired colour is achieved.

Bronze disease is a form of corrosion that attacks ancient bronzes and, unless checked, can cause considerable damage. It manifests itself in small spots whose colour is usually light green. Cures for bronze disease involve soaking for long periods of time in clean water or strong solution of sodium sequicarbonate.

BUHL

Andre Charles Boulle was the man who developed the highly ornate brass, tortoiseshell and ebony inlay fashionable in France during the latter part of the seventeenth century.

Being expensive furniture, it is usually fairly well cared for and by far the commonest repairs are those involving replacement of missing pieces of inlay. These are always rather involved shapes and difficult to recut from the proper materials. Wax and sealing wax are therefore the easiest materials with which to effect repairs.

Since tortoiseshell is never a single colour, a few sticks of sealing wax will

Three 19th century bronze figures — their fine patination adds to their values and should not be interfered with. (King & Chasemore)

A fine 19th century buhl centre table. yellow wax, tortoiseshell with sealing wax.

Missing brass can be simulated with

be required, ranging in colour from pale yellow to black and it would be advisable to try a few practice blobs before tackling the actual job.

It is usually best to start with the black and build up the paler colours around and above it, rubbing down with fine sandpaper to obtain a smooth surface. Streaks and blotches resembling the actual tortoiseshell are much easier to obtain than might be thought.

Having established the tortoiseshell areas and rubbed them down level with the surrounding surface, drip yellow wax into the places where brass is missing and finish off by polishing well. If any areas are too bright, tone them down with a little brown shoe polish.

CANDLE WAX

Candle wax drippings can be removed from furniture by scraping gently with a razor blade.

Most fabrics can be effectively treated by ironing them between sheets

of brown paper (keep applying fresh brown paper so as not to transfer the wax back again to different parts of the fabric). A little chloroform or carbon bisulphide will effectively remove any remaining traces.

CANEWORK

Very often, the only thing wrong with canework is that it is dirty. Warm soapy water and sunshine are two of the best cleansers. Give it a good scrub with soapy water and leave it to dry in the sunshine — this has a slight bleaching effect. If the canework is badly stained, resort to using a weak solution of household bleach but be sure to wash away all traces afterwards, for bleach will tend to rot the cane if left on.

After cleaning, re-thread unravelled pieces and stick them down with Evostik Resin W. When everything is thoroughly dry, a coat of matt finish polyurethane will protect it without that hideously false high gloss effect. An alternative finish can be made by shaving beeswax and dissolving it in benzene to a brushable consistency, applying a good coat and finishing with a brisk rub with a lint free duster.

CARPETS

The important thing to remember about carpets is that some of them are worth a great deal of money and, being made of organic material, are liable to rot or unravel unless treated with due care.

Never, therefore, wet a carpet so thoroughly that the back becomes soaked, and always check for colour fastness before attempting any cleaning or stain removal.

To test colour fastness, lay a sheet of white blotting paper under an inconspicuous corner of the carpet and moisten the pile with warm soapy water. Always use distilled water or rainwater, particularly on carpets which may be valuable, since all tap water contains a certain amount of bleaching chemical.

For the treatment of small areas, colours can be fixed by application of a 5% solution of common salt.

For general washing, use a cloth or brush moistened with a little warm soapy water — Fairy Liquid or other washing up liquid is quite satisfactory — and brush with the lay of the pile. To brush against the pile could cause certain hand-knotted carpets to have their knots loosened.

A good treatment for stains is to mix up fullers' earth into a thick paste with distilled water, smearing this onto the affected area and leaving it to dry thoroughly before brushing it out.

Oily marks will benefit from having dry talcum powder brushed well in. Sawdust, too, worked into the pile and brushed out again will be found to bring a great deal of dirt away and will even be found to have an effect on tea and coffee stains.

White spirit and oil of pine are two solvents that may be used with care to remove stains. The latter should be kept in a well stoppered, dark bottle to prevent sticky resins from forming.

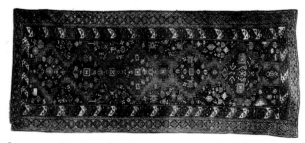

A good Kazak rug — always seek advice before cleaning valuable carpets and rugs. (King & Chasemore)

CHALK DRAWINGS & PASTELS

Chalk drawings and pastels, are of an extremely delicate nature and are best left to expert hands for repairs and restorative work.

Under no circumstances should the surface ever be touched — even after being treated with a fixative spray — and framing should always be done in such a way that there is clear space between the drawing and the glass.

CHANDELIERS

Crystal chandeliers should be carefully dismantled before cleaning.

Chandeliers have been made of just about every possible material and combination of materials from wood and iron to antlers. Most, however, are of brass and glass.

By virtue of their siting, chandeliers are not normally susceptible to damage — except when they are taken down for cleaning. The first rule is never to attempt to take down a chandelier unaided.

The best way of cleaning most chandeliers is to dismantle them and clean each piece individually according to the material of which it is made. This can be the most tedious of tasks, particularly in the case of crystal chandeliers. As a precautionary measure, study the disposition of the pieces carefully to ensure that you remember how to reassemble them!

Not infrequently, the wire pins and hooks which hold the chandelier together will be found to be so corroded that they break during dismantling. Replacements can be bought from glass stockists and some hardware shops, or they can be made from copper or brass wire.

Missing crystals are often difficult to match exactly, but most antiques dealers have a stock of odd pieces which may match nearly enough — small discrepancies will hardly be noticed once the chandelier has been rehung.

For other repairs, see other headings relating to the material from which the chandelier is made.

Brass chandeliers will stay clean for years if properly lacquered.

CHINA

China is no exception to the rule that cleaning must always precede repair.

Sturdy pieces will stand being washed in a bowl of warm water with just a little detergent added. It is always wise to take precautions against accidents when washing china and a piece of foam rubber in the bottom of the bowl can do nothing but good. It is always best, too, to remove the washing up bowl from the sink so that a moment's inattention will not cause a piece of precious china to be banged against the taps.

Fragile pieces will be better cleaned by wiping them gently with cotton wool or a sable brush moistened with soapy water or, if stained, with a solution of hydrogen peroxide. Tea and coffee stains in cups or saucers will yield to a solution of salt or bicarbonate of soda.

Old pieces will often be found to have been previously repaired with adhesives which have turned brown. These are best re-repaired and a soak in hot water will soften most old glues (being usually based on animal products — horn, hoof or hide) while others will almost certainly give way to acetone or meths. Remember, however, that the glue has to be penetrated and this may necessitate fairly prolonged soaking before it is softened sufficiently to allow the pieces to be parted.

Absolutely all traces of old glue must be thoroughly removed from china before repairs are attempted. The whole technique of china repair is to bring the pieces to be joined into the closest possible contact and even the tiniest speck of foreign matter can render this impossible and result in an unsightly, gappy join.

Once all pieces are completely clean, try fitting them dry to make sure that no more than the finest hairline can be seen. If this is not the case, there must be some traces of foreign matter in the way — use a magnifying glass if necessary to inspect the edges and pick out foreign matter with a fine needle.

Although they have great strength, epoxy resin adhesives are rarely to be recommended for china repair. If, as sometimes happens, the pieces move during sticking they will need to be parted and rejoined — an extremely difficult task if the adhesive is as hard and strong as Araldite, for instance (though even this is said to be soluble if Dissolvex is used). Better, then, are the clear acetate adhesives which are thin enough to permit a close join without unduly sacrificing strength.

The important thing to remember when gluing china is not to be caught on the hop once the pieces have been glued and brought into contact. Make sure that you know where the pieces are going to be put and how they will be held tightly in place while the adhesive sets. A useful aid here is a box filled with dry sand or a quantity of putty or plasticene. A roll of sticky tape is an essential for most jobs.

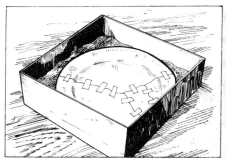

Squeeze out a quantity of adhesive onto a sheet of glass and, with a clean finger, spread as thin a film as possible on the edges to be joined, working it well into crevices and taking care not to cut yourself on the sometimes sharp edges. As soon as both surfaces are coated, press them as firmly as common sense allows into contact, moving them slightly to ensure that they fit absolutely tightly. Wipe off the beads of excess glue which ooze from the join.

Use plenty of sticky tape to hold the pieces together while the glue sets, running the tape in lengths across the join and at right angles to it. Once this is done, prop the piece on the putty or plasticine, or in the dry sand, in such a way that gravity does not tend to pull the join apart.

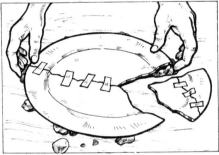

There are many arguments waged about the suitability of different types of adhesive tape to be used for holding glued pieces together while they set, one school of thought maintaining that the brown paper type is to be preferred above all because of its tendency to shrink while it is drying, the opposite school insisting that sellotape is easier to clean off afterwards and, anyway, the amount of shrinkage of the tape is unlikely to help the join at all.

Since most of the clear sticky tapes are slightly elastic, it would seem that they offer the best of both worlds, being decidedly easier to remove.

Pieces that are broken in several places should be rebuilt a piece at a time, making sure that the last piece can be placed in position.

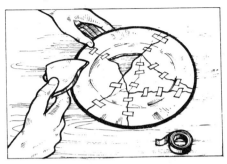

Many old repairs were carried out using ugly metal rivets set into specially drilled holes, the overall effect being to impart to the piece a kind of Frankensteinian appearance. These can now be removed, thanks to strong modern adhesives, and the drill holes filled with one of the many china pastes available. Where preferred, a china paste can be made using Araldite mixed with marble dust or kaolin to a really stiff paste. This should be applied so that it stands proud of the surrounding surface and then, after twenty four hours, rubbed gently down with scalpel, needle files and wet or dry paper, taking care not to scratch the surrounding glaze.

Chips and missing sections can be built up using the same method and quite intricate patterns can be reproduced with care.

Once the paste has been taken down to the right level, it should be coloured to blend in with the rest of the piece. Artists oils can be used or, better, finely ground dry colours mixed with water-clear synthetic varnish. White will be found to be the hardest colour to match. Paint should be kept as thin as possible consistent with adequate covering power. Applied too thickly, it will leave unsightly ridges, too thinly and the filler colour will show through.

Missing pieces can be made for china ornaments fairly simply by modelling them in plasticene or other medium and making casts of either plaster or the Araldite filler described above.

For accuracy's sake, it is probably best to make the plasticene replacement member actually on the object being repaired.

This really is not too difficult to do and, if you are hesitant about attempting it, remember that nothing at all can be lost and much gained by making the effort.

Having made a replica of the missing piece, remove it carefully from the body of the object and carefully insert a small rod into one end (or both if it is a large piece) in such a way that the piece can be supported horizontally on it.

On the sheet of glass, build a wall of clay (or plasticene will do) large enough to surround your model with about an inch of clear space all round.

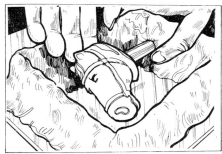

Support your model, using the rod pushed into the wall of clay, so that its lower edge is at least half an inch clear of the glass.

Very lightly, mark the middle line of your model.

Mix a quantity of plaster of paris to the consistency of cream (making sure

there are no lumps) and pour this immediately into the mould until its surfaces just reaches your marked centre line.

When the plaster has set, carve two or more grooves into the surface, making sure that they are not undercut.

Coat the plaster thoroughly with soft soap and, mixing a fresh quantity pour this over your model to the top of the wall of clay. The soft soap will stop the fresh plaster from sticking to the old.

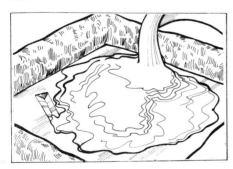

When this second pouring has set, the clay is stripped away, the two parts of the mould prized apart and the model removed.

All being well, you should now have a perfect mould of your plasticene model. The grooves will be matched by keys to ensure that the mould will go together in correct alignment and, where

the model met the wall of clay, there will be a hole.

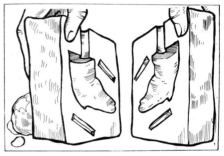

Once again, the plaster is thoroughly soft soaped and the two halves of the mould tied firmly together with

string. More plaster is mixed and this is poured into the hole in the mould.

Shake and tap the mould quite vigorously to ensure that all air bubbles are driven out. When the plaster has set, part the mould and, presto! a new piece for your broken ornament.

A better piece can be made — in terms of strength — by using Araldite china filler as described above in place of plaster for the final cast. Silicone grease must be used instead of soft soap in this case as a parting agent. The filler should be pressed firmly into the mould and pushed well down to ensure that it fills every crevice. Leave it for twenty four hours to harden before parting the mould.

Once the new piece has been removed from the mould, a certain amount of work will probably prove necessary — removal of the flash etc. — before it is affixed to the ornament. Any discrep-

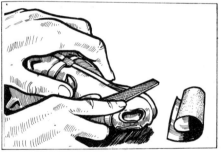

ancies in fit can be either built up with more filler or filed carefully away. Once glued into position, the new piece can be coloured to match.

New handles for cups, vases and jugs can be made in the same way, but

these are better if they contain wire braces through their centres which should, ideally, extend for about 1/8 inch either end and be fitted into holes carefully drilled into the remaining stubs. The drilling of these holes is a tricky business and not to be recommended to those who are neither handy with tools nor lucky. Special, diamond tipped bits can be bought from good toolshops and the object must be held absolutely steady while drilling is in progress to prevent chipping and flaking.

There are on the market, a variety or rubberised moulding materials which may be used instead of plaster of paris. These can usually be obtained from good art shops, particularly those which specialise in handicrafts or sculpture supplies. Their great advantages are that they do not chip or break and they can be used to take mouldings of originals which must not be damaged.

Using one of these materials, a stock of moulds can be built up of hands, faces, knobs and other frequently-missing pieces against the day they are needed. Since their application varies from type to type, it would be pointless to describe their various methods, particularly since manufacturers' instructions are generally given with the preparations.

When repairing china ornaments, a degree of creativity is often required

to conceal joins. Common dodges are to conceal neck joins with necklaces, wrist joins with bracelets, leg joins with garters — all built up slightly with filler.

The figure on the right has had its arm badly repaired. The join could have been concealed by the addition of a bracelet.

CHRONOMETERS

A chronometer is a clock or watch of great precision and accuracy. The usual application of the term, as regards antiques, is a ship's timepiece and these are normally fitted into sturdy boxes — often with the lids removed.

Where repairs to clock or watch movements should rarely be attempted by the amateur, those to chronometers should always be left to the professional. Cleaning up and repairs to the external parts, of course, are simple enough to be tackled by anyone and will greatly enhance the appearance of the piece.

The commonest repair entails filling up the holes left in the wooden box by removal of the lid (which is often missing by the time a chronometer reaches the market). The rebates cut for the hinges can be plugged by cutting strips of the appropriate timber and gluing these into position before matching the colour to that of the rest of the box and polishing. The lock is usually left in place and it is a matter of choice whether this is unscrewed and its rebate filled, or whether it is simply polished up and lacquered.

A beautifully kept ship's chronometer by Edward Baker of London.
(King & Chasemore)

CIGARETTE BURNS

Some mention of methods of repairing cigarette burns on furniture has been made under the section headed **Bleaching**

When the depressions made by burns are particularly deep, all charred wood must be removed and the surface brought back to the surrounding level of wood. This is done with either an epoxy resin filler (which has the advantage of hardness but does not take a high gloss when polished) or with a wax stick, shellac stick or a plug of the appropriate wood.

Using a small, sharp chisel, cut away the small amount of wood necessary to remove all traces of scorching from top and front surfaces. Undercut the sides and back to ensure that any wax, resin or shellac filler will key well in and not fall out the first time the area is polished. With luck,

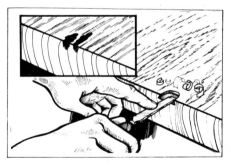

it will not be necessary to remove the finish from surrounding wood if wax or shellac are used for the repair.

The choice of filler will depend largely on the size of the space to be filled. Wax is really only suitable for quite small repairs, particularly on an edge. Shellac, although not as durable as resin, should be quite suitable for most repairs, particularly in areas which do not receive much wear. Resin is the hardest of all but, as has been

mentioned, this does not take a high gloss, though some success has been achieved in this direction by coating a piece of glass carefully with parting agent and pressing this into contact with the resin as it cures.

A more permanent repair — and more difficult — involves using a piece of wood instead of wax or shellac to replace the timber cut away in the removal of burn marks.

The place is prepared in exactly the same way as described above, and a small plug of the appropriate wood is cut to fit precisely into the cavity. This will be simplified if the hole is not undercut.

Finishing will be greatly simplified if the new wood can be matched closely to the old for colour and grain. Where this is not possible, use a piece lighter in colour than the table top, since it is always easier to darken wood than lighten it.

The plug of wood is glued into position and rubbed carefully down flush with the surrounding timber once the glue has set. Any variations of colour can now be adjusted and the patch polished to blend with the rest of the piece (see Polishing).

A fine longcase clock, in a Chippendale-style mahogany case. (Henry Spencer & Sons).

CLOCKS

When a clock stops working it may be that a vital part has broken or become badly worn. Very often, however, the problem is much simpler — a build-up of gummy dust in the works which is clogging them and preventing free movement.

Having looked into the back of the clock to see that there is nothing obviously preventing the mechanism from pursuing its predetermined course, open the front and make sure that the hands are able to turn freely without catching either on each other or on the face. If it is a chiming clock, allow the chimes to run their full course each time the hands pass go.

If the clock has a movement driven by weights, check to see that these are running freely on their pulleys — replace broken or worn gut with nylon cord or fresh gut. Do not use cotton or any other natural fibre cord since this is inclined to wear and produce fluff which finds its way into the works of the clock and cause the kind of build-up we are talking about.

If none of the above activities improves the clock's performance, the moment has come to make a decision — to have it repaired professionally or to pursue your own endeavours further. If the clock has any value it really should be taken to a clockmaker who is qualified to do the job. These, alas, are quite hard to find, most High Street shops relying for their success on repairs to modern, mass produced movements whose parts can be replaced from stock.

Assuming that the clock is more or less of the old banger variety and you are determined to attempt restoring it to life yourself, first remove the mechanism from its case.

Remove the hands first; sometimes they will pull straight off, others are held in place by a tapered steel pin or piece of wire.

Most mechanisms are held in their cases by screws which are undone from the back, sometimes, however, these screws are located behind the face, in which case the face will also be held in place by means of screws which are undone from the front.

The mechanism will lift out of the case in one piece and, to clean it of gummed up oil and dirt, simply swish it about in a bowl of petrol, working at stubborn lumps with a brush or feather. Needless to say, this should be done outdoors and the usual fire precautions should be taken.

Once removed from the petrol, the mechanism will quickly dry by evaporation and it should now be minimally lubricated with a few drops of light oil applied to the bearings with a fine brush or a feather – **squirt cans are useless for this job since they always deliver too much oil at once and this is precisely what must be avoided.**

While applying the oil, check cogs for movement. If they rock from side to side, their bearings are worn and in need of attention by an experienced repair man.

Before replacing the movement, any necessary repairs can be carried out to the case. The interior should be thoroughly cleaned of dust and, if there are any splits in the woodwork, they should be repaired if only for the reason that they allow dirt and dust to enter the works. The least repair would be to stick brown paper tape over them from the inside. If they are clean and not too narrow, splits can be made good by glueing in strips of the appropriate veneer which should be left standing proud until the glue has set and then

19th century French buhl bracket clock. (Henry Spencer & Sons).

An exceptionally fine bracket clock, by Daniel Quare in an ebonised case 11½ins high. Such clocks as these should be professionally repaired.

pared down to the level of the surrounding surface with scalpel and fine sandpaper, finally being stained and polished to blend in. Other cracks can be filled with a wax stick.

Many clocks have, in their sides or back, brass grilles or pierced panels covered on the inside with silk. This will probably need replacing as it tends to rot with age. Its purpose is to prevent dust from flowing freely into the works while allowing air to circulate and the chimes to sound out clear and unmuffled.

Chipped enamel faces can be filled with white china filler which will probably need to be painted if its colour is to match. Some people obtain black and white photographic copies of clock faces which, since they are normally seen behind glass, escape detection quite well.

Once-blued hands which have rusted should be rubbed down gently with the finest grade of wet or dry paper and then reblued with any of the proprietary preparations available for the purpose. An alternative colouring treatment is to blacken them in the soot from a candle flame and fix this with a spray lacquer.

Brass work should be cleaned with metal polish and relacquered. If, as is so often the case, the brass has been lacquered, this can be removed with meths first. Plain steel parts should be rubbed free of rust after which they will respond favourably to treatment with ordinary black shoe polish.

Pendulum clocks need setting carefully if they are to work properly. They must stand on a firm base and they must stand level. The time interval between tick and tock must be the same and this is a matter for adjustment. Tilt the clock slightly until the time interval is the same and then, opening the back, bend the crutch gently toward the side of the clock that was raised. More bending or less may be needed to set the pendulum correctly; once set, the clock should not be moved.

To regulate the clock, raise or lower the pendulum bob by means of the screw beneath it. The shorter the distance between the bob and its support, the faster the clock will go.

Missing keys are generally not too difficult to replace but, in the event that this is impossible or that a temporary key is needed, it is quite a simple matter to make a new one. Obtain a short length of copper or brass tubing whose internal diameter is no larger than the diagonal across the winding spigot. Tap one end of the tube square with a small hammer and cut a slot in the other into which a cross piece can be soldered. This can be as plain or elaborate as you care to make it.

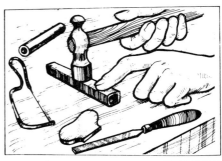

CLOTHES MOTHS

A cream silk wedding dress, circa 1870. (King & Chasemore).

The larvae of the clothes moth (tinea trapezana) feed on fur, feathers, hair and wool, wreaking havoc and destruction wherever they go.

Prevention being the best cure, it is as well to remember that these grubs are unlikely to be found in garments which are shaken out and aired regularly or in carpets and rugs which are frequently brushed or cleaned.

Objects and materials likely to be attractive to clothes moths should be stored in a mothproof container with mothballs or a few paradichlorbenzene crystals.

Rentokil supply a mothproofing preparation in the form of a spray which is lethal to a variety of other creatures including carpet beetles.

COINS AND MEDALS

Coins are found in a variety of metals and, generally, are best cleaned only when absolutely necessary, particularly if they are made of silver.

A five percent solution of nitric acid is recommended for the occasional cleaning of most coins and medals, these being immersed for only one or two seconds in the solution before being immediately washed in running water and gently dried. Great care must be taken since prolonged or frequent exposure to nitric acid will result in the metal being etched.

Old coins are sometimes encrusted with limestone or other mineral deposits. To remove these, coat any visible areas of metal with wax and immerse the coins in nitric. acid — it may be found that a more concentrated solution than that used for cleaning will be needed, even full strength acid being required in some cases. Watch carefully as treatment progresses, bearing in mind that any exposed metal will suffer as a result of prolonged contact with the acid. Remove the items from the bath from time to time and scrape at the mineral deposits with a bone or plastic knitting needle, covering each fresh area of exposed metal with wax before returning it to the bath. Remember that nitric acid is very dangerous — any which gets onto the skin should immediately be flooded off with plenty of running water.

Gold is best cleaned with soap, water and stiff brush.

Silver coins really are best left uncleaned if their value is not to be impaired. Carbon tetrachloride or trichlorethylene gently applied will remove greasy dirt and should be washed off immediately after treatment. Goddard's

Silver Dip will improve some discolourations but silver coins should never be polished or rubbed — a polished shine is disapproved of in collecting circles.

After cleaning, protect coins and medals with a thinly applied wax polish.

COPPER AND BRASS

Copper and brass objects seem generally to be found either highly polished or totally filthy. The first offers no problems, the second not too many.

As a rule it is a waste of time to attack filthily discoloured copper and brass with metal polish — the most you are likely to achieve is an object covered in highly polished dirt.

Diluted ammonia is generally recommended to remove dirt and grease from the surface of brass but ammonia is such foul stuff to work with that a good strong detergent may well prove a preferable substitute.

Having removed the superficial layers of dirt, it will be found necessary to clean the brass of stains and discolourations of the metal itself. A weak acid and salt solution is ideal for this, and either oxalic acid or vinegar can be used equally effectively; a couple of tablespoons of vinegar (or one of saturated solution of oxalic acid) to one heaped tablespoon of salt dissolved in a pint of water should prove to be about the right proportions.

After treatment with acid and salt, the piece should be clean but there may still be some nasty, corroded spots or patches which will simply have to be rubbed away with find sandpaper — use this sparingly, remembering that it will scratch the surface of the brass and cause considerable extra work if a good, polished finish is to be restored.

Copper requires slightly different cleaning methods than those used for brass. A paste of powdered chalk and meths makes a good general cleanser which removes most corrosion and stains quite simply. This is followed by a good rub with crocus powder or whiting, and any proprietary metal polish will finish the job.

An alternative method is to cut a lemon in half, dip it in salt and rub the object with this — the acid from the lemon acting as a substitute for the weak vinegar used for cleaning brass.

Broken pieces can be repaired either by soldering them or by means of an epoxy resin. The first method has the advantage of being more traditional, and soldered repairs are not too unsightly on highly polished pieces. The epoxy resin method is simpler and very effective if the piece is not highly polished or the repair is in a place which is not too prominent.

Hard solder, or spelter, is used to repair brass.

First clean thoroughly the area to be soldered, filing and abrading it until all traces of dirt, grease and corrosion are removed.

Apply flux to the metal and set the pieces together.

Lay spelter along the break and, with a small blow lamp, gently heat both object and spelter until the latter runs and fuses with the surrounding metal.

The epoxy resin method involves the use of a resin such as Araldite and to fill holes, a quantity of brass powder filler which can be bought at good art and sculpture suppliers.

Simple breaks are glued in the usual manner.

Holes are filled by mixing up a sufficient quantity of Araldite and add ing to it enough brass powder to make a stiff paste.

If the hole is of any size, a support of some kind will be needed to prevent

the resin mixture from sagging while it sets. Hollow objects can be stuffed with newspaper, and a piece of glass fibre mat coated with resin and laid across from the inside.

When this has set, mix the brass powder-filled resin and work it in, making sure that the mixture stands proud of the surrounding metal.

When it is quite hard, this can be rubbed down to blend with the surrounding surface and polished.

CRACKS IN WOOD

There are three methods of repairing splits in wood and each has its uses and misuses. The split can be filled with veneer, shellac or wax; it can be pushed shut and held in place by means of a piece of wood fixed across it or it can be glued under pressure.

If the split is fairly short and narrow, particularly if it is in the top of an old piece of furniture or in a place which would be difficult to repair by any other method, the thing to do is to simply fill it up with wax, shellac or pieces of veneer.

Wax or shellac coloured to match the surrounding wood can be dripped

into the split and polished to blend in.

Strips of veneer can be glued into the split then rubbed down, stained and polished.

Split Panels which would be difficult to remove from their appointed places are best repaired by the second method.

Using a thin bladed knife, run round the edges of the panel to make sure that it is not fixed to the surrounding frame anywhere. The two broken sections can then be pushed together without let or hindrance. This is absolutely essential; if the panel is not free to move in its frame, it will split again as often as it is repaired.

Clean the broken sides of the split as best you can and run in a little glue.

Push the panel together and, working from the back, glue strips of thin wood (or a single, long strip) across the split.

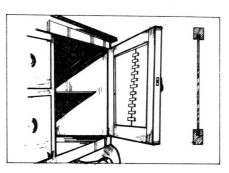

With a damp cloth, wipe all excess glue from the front of the panel and apply pressure to the patches.

When the glue has set, rub wax into the crack from the front.

To Repair a Split in a Table Top, Chest Top, or any other large, Solid Piece of Wood:

If the wood is not split along its

entire length, break it so that you have two separate pieces.

Clean the broken edges of the wood thoroughly to remove all grease and dirt but do not remove any wood. (i.e. do not use sandpaper or scraping tools — only solvents if these are necessary).

If you have no sash cramps, prepare an area of floor next to a wall by screwing down a piece of wood (at least as long as the piece to be repaired). This should be fixed parallel to the wall and just far enough away that the repaired piece will fit between it and the wall with no more than an inch or two to spare.

Lay paper on the floor between this and the wall.

Cut a couple of long wedges.

Glue the broken edges of the wood to be repaired and lay them, face up, between the wall and your screwed-down batten.

Protecting the edge of your repair with a thin strip of wood, drive the wedges between this and the screwed-down batten to force the glued edges of your repair into close contact. Take care that the two pieces do not spring up in the middle.

With a damp cloth, wipe away any squeezed out glue from the surface of the wood and apply weights around the join to ensure that it lays flat.

When the glue has set, knock out the wedges, remove the weights and repaired piece of wood. The paper laid on the floor will doubtless be sticking to the back; this can be scraped off.

Refix the piece of wood to its original position.

Restain and polish as necessary.

If the split piece was the centre section of a drop-leaf table, it may be found that the sides no longer hang properly. An inspection of the underside will probably reveal that they are fouling on the corners of the swivelling legs. To rectify this, simply cut away some of the wood from the undersides of the offending leaves with either a chisel or a coarse sanding disc on a rotary sander.

CUTLERY

As everyone knows, washing cutlery in too-hot water loosens handles. Sometimes they come right off, sometimes they just seem to work their way up the tangs, leaving unsightly (and unhygienic), black gaps.

As always, effective repairs demand thorough cleaning.

Remove the handle completely from the tang and clean off all the old adhesive (frequently natural resin) from both tang and interior of the handle. The latter task is rather tedious but can be simplified by using a drill bit of exactly the right diameter in a wheel-brace, taking care to drill straight and not widen the hole.

Either resin of the natural kind or epoxy resin can be used to refix handles, the latter being the easiest and safest method. Normally, the hollow in the handle would be nearly filled with Araldite and the tang pushed fully home; all excess, squeezed-out adhesive being removed before it reaches full hardness.

If, however, the handle is split, or if the adhesive will be visible after the repair is finished, it should be mixed with a suitably pigmented filler powder.

Natural resin is a more traditional adhesive for the job.

The cleaned-out cavity is filled with melted resin and the tang is brought to red heat and pushed full home.

Remember, if attempting this for the first time, that the tang must be pushed in absolutely straight and clean — in one go. Remember, too, that the handle is going to become very hot during the operation and must be held in a vice or other suitable clamp. Naturally, any contact between the heated tang and the outside surface of the handle will result in an unsightly (and probably ineradicable) burn mark.

DENTS IN WOOD

If dents occur in the softer woods (including mahogany), there is a good chance that they can be steamed out. Harder woods such as oak and rosewood are unlikely to respond to treatment and dents will have to be filled.

The principle behind the effectiveness of steaming dents is that, by forcing moisture into the fibres of the wood they will be obliged to swell and, hopefully, resume their former positions and sizes.

First, all polish or other finish must be removed from the dent and a reasonably large surrounding area. Since chest and table tops are the parts most likely to be treated, this usually means stripping off the entire surface in order to obtain an even colour and finish upon completion of the job.

A wet cloth pad is placed over the dent and a hot iron applied with heavy hand pressure.

This is repeated several times, making sure that the pad is kept well soaked.

After this, the iron is turned down to warm and simply left standing on the wet pad for as long as necessary — possibly several hours — and again, the pad must not be allowed to dry out.

When the dent is out, leave the piece for a couple of days to dry out naturally before sanding, staining and repolishing.

A simpler method (and the only one for hard woods) is to fill the depression with melted shellac of the right colour, sanding down afterwards to cut the shellac back to the level of the encircling wood. This must be done with the aid of a largish sanding block if the finished repair is to be flat.

DOLLS

Dolls have been made of many different materials, from wood to wax and, while some are simple and robust, others are extraordinarily delicate and complicated in their construction.

Naturally enough, very few dolls have survived their original use in perfect condition, almost all being likely to benefit from some careful attention, and it is this which accounts in some measure for the high value of rarer examples.

It is perhaps worth considering that, as a general rule, Araldite and other epoxy resin adhesives should never be used by amateurs to join broken parts of dolls; only adhesives for which there are really effective solvents should be employed for this purpose, though the epoxy resins are invaluable for making new parts which can be fixed in place with gentler adhesives when they are set.

Because of the way they were made, probably the commonest complaints from which dolls suffer are broken or disconnected heads and limbs. Since these are often of china or bisque, breaks and missing parts are dealt with in the same way as ordinary china, being carefully glued and re-modelled using a clear acetate adhesive and a good china filler.

Disconnected limbs are usually rejoined by means of elastic which invariably follows a similar threading pattern to that illustrated. A long up-

holstery needle or crochet hook is a useful tool for threading the elastic through the hollow body of the doll but, in the absence of either of these, sellotape the elastic onto the end of a knitting needle and use that. Short lengths of wire bent into S or C shapes are useful for hooking the elastic onto the loops of the doll, allowing the elastic to be knotted before it is put into place.

A doll with moveable eyes will invariably be found to have a cardboard crown to its head concealed under the wig. Repairs to the eye mechanism are

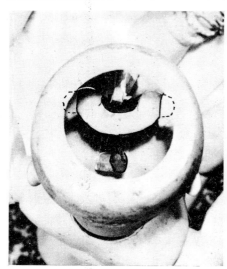

made from inside the head after wig and crown have been carefully removed. Missing eyes are, of course, a problem — specialist suppliers being hard to find. Painted beads can be used, but only as a last resort. If the bridge onto which the eyes are fastened is broken, rebuild it with a strong china paste or epoxy resin.

It is not uncommon to find that the domed joints containing the loops through which the elastic is threaded are missing or broken. These can sometimes be replaced with blazer-type buttons. For the head, use a button considerably larger than the hole and rely on the pull of the elastic to hold it in place. Elsewhere, the buttons will probably have to be glued in place, so it is best to use leather, plastic or wooden buttons rather than those of metal.

Wigs are often thin and tangled. Replacements are almost impossible to buy and remaking a wig is a task to tax the patience of a saint. Tangles must be combed out very carefully indeed, a few hairs at a time, starting at the bottom and working upward. If the wig is so thin that bald patches show through, a ribbon or a hat will have to be used to disguise the spots.

Fortunately, it is possible to buy a small hair piece made to fit over a bun. An old wig or larger hair piece might be cut down quite successfully and threaded with elastic to hold it in place.

Repainting is best done with artists' oil colours or the acrylic paints which are available through art shops and which dry in a few minutes. Because colouring varies from doll to doll, it would be pointless here to attempt to give precise colour details. In general, however, colours should be applied in thin, transparent coats to build up the clear, glowing tints which look so clean and attractive. Flesh colour is not made by mixing red and white into a more or less sickly pink. It is built up in layers starting with white, shaded thinly with grey and blue. A transparent yellow is laid over this and then a very thin coat of crimson is applied. It is important that every coat should be as thin as possible so as to permit the underlying colours to show through. All those horrible, putty coloured faces are the result of paints mixed ad lib and applied thickly and without care.

Some dolls will be found to be made of a kind of papier mache compound. This is best repaired with a material of like nature made by shredding old newspapers into water and then either leaving them to soak or boiling them to a pulp. Add a little paste — polycell is fine — and squeeze out excess moisture. Press the resultant mess into the holes, leaving it to stand proud of the surrounding area until it has dried (overnight in the airing cupboard should be long enough) when it can be rubbed down with sandpaper and coloured to match.

Wax dolls are extremely difficult to repair. They can be cleaned with a little cold cream on cotton wool swabs and small cracks can be gently worked over with a little turps. This demands the greatest care, since turps softens the wax and a too liberal application or rough handling can do irreparable harm. Turps will also remove any paint from the surface of the wax, and although some wax dolls are coloured from within, many will need to have new features painted on after treatment with it.

Be very wary of trying to repair wax dolls with melted candle wax — this is so rarely successful that it is really not worth attempting.

DRAWERS

Assuming we are talking about furniture that has been reasonably well put together, drawers only stick for three reasons: Wet, Warp or Wear.

Before dealing with specific remedies for sticking drawers, it would be as well to examine the way in which drawers work and the effects of wet, warp and wear on them — an understanding which will make the diagnosis of a drawer's ills far easier.

A drawer is simply a tray which slides into an aperture in a piece of furniture in order to save space and keep things tidy. In order to fulfil this function properly, the sides of the drawer (and of the aperture) must be parallel, straight and reasonably close fitting.

Some drawers are made to slide upon runners — wooden slats, usually fixed to the sides of the aperture, which run in grooves cut in the sides of the drawer (occasionally the slats are fixed to the drawer sides and run on ledges inside the aperture). Other drawers simply slide in and out, their sides resting on the bottom of the aperture.

If, for any reason, the sides of the drawer cease to be parallel to each other or to the sides of the aperture, sticking is likely to occur.

Since drawers are always fitted individually to their apertures, it is essential that each drawer should be in the right place. Newly acquired pieces should therefore be checked to make sure that this is so. If the drawers stick, swap them about before embarking on more drastic measures.

Because of the lack of air circulation within a piece of furniture, damp is most likely to manifest itself within the carcase. Drawers, being made to fit nicely when dry, are inclined to stick if they swell even slightly. The first thing to check then, if a drawer sticks, is the wetness of the wood.

The obvious remedy if damp is suspected is to move the entire piece of furniture to a drier place. Failing this, remove the drawers regularly and allow them to dry out. If the sticking is not too bad, apply soap or candle wax to the areas at which sticking occurs. **Do not remove any of the wood from the drawer or its runners** since this will cause trouble later if the piece is moved to a dry place.

Damp can also cause warping and, when this happens, some wood will have to be removed in order to cure the trouble.

Take the drawer completely out of the carcase and look along each side to see if there is any bowing. Look too, for shiny patches on the sides, since these will indicate where the friction causing the sticking is taking place. Sand, scrape or plane these areas back a little and rub them over with candle wax.

If the drawer is of the type which runs on runners, look along these to make sure that they are not bowed. If they are, they will have to be replaced, particularly if the curve is up and down.

Inspection for warp will also reveal any signs of wear. If the load bearing surfaces have become badly worn, the drawer will be inclined to fit sloppily and move unevenly as it is opened and closed. Sometimes runners are so badly worn that the drawer slips completely off them and tends to fall into the interior of the carcase. There is no alternative to replacing worn runners.

If the drawer does not run on runners but on small blocks of wood glued underneath, check these for wear and replace them if necessary.

Although it would seem at first that wear should allow drawers to move more freely, it must be remembered that very few people actually push drawers straight in; pressure is usually applied more to one side than the other, causing the drawer to jam as diagonally opposite corners are forced against the sides of the aperture. Candle wax or soap applied to the sliding and jamming surfaces will ease the problem but the real answer is always to replace worn parts.

EBONISED FURNITURE

When repairs are made to ebonised furniture, one of the most difficult tasks is matching the particular black used on the surrounding timber.

Black shoe dye is often used with success — two or more applications sometimes being necessary to obtain the correct density. Sometimes the black will be found to need the addition of some dark blue or dark brown to correct colour. Black emulsion paint, too can be used to good effect.

Whichever method is used to obtain the colour, the piece should be allowed to dry and then given a coat of french polish. This, too, will have an effect on the colour, and it is a good idea to make a few experimental attempts first.

ENAMEL

It is important that the distinction be made between true enamel and the enamel paints sold all over the place. True enamel is essentially a type of coloured glass, applied as a paste and then fired to fuse it to the base on which it has been put. In order that the firing process should not cause adjacent colours to fuse and run together, two main techniques are used; Cloisonne and Champleve.

A slightly restored cloisonne enamel ovoid vase of the K'ang Hsi period. (King & Chasemore).

Cloisonne enamels are made by soldering fine wires onto the surface of the base in such a way that the pattern is divided into small cells, each of which is filled with the coloured paste. After firing, the wires remain visible and form part of the design.

Champleve enamels are made by cutting depressions actually into the metal base and filling these with the enamel paste, the walls of the depressions preventing a flow of colours during firing.

Sometimes, an enamel base is prepared and used as a ground for further painting (painted enamel), while the plique a jour technique involves the use of wires in the same manner as the cloisonne but, after firing, the metal base is removed.

In all cases repair is difficult. Prior cleaning should be done with the greatest care in warm, soapy water using only the softest of brushes.

In cases where the enamel is parting from its metal base, immersion in Canada balsam dissolved in benzole is recommended. Missing fragments can be replaced by suitably coloured epoxy resin or celluloid. The latter is prepared by dissolving it in amyl acetate until it forms a fairly stiff, syrupy mass which can be coloured and applied to the clean metal base and left to dry.

Since neither epoxy resin nor celluloid are 100% satisfactory for restoring enamel, many workers consider that good quality oil colours can be used as effectively as either.

As an alternative repair technique, a thin acrylic varnish applied fairly liberally to the entire piece will do good work in holding loose and flaking pieces of enamel in place. Once dry, this should be wiped over with a cotton wool swab just moistened with acetone.

Great care must be taken here, otherwise the acetone will simply undo all the work done by the acrylic.

Once all loose pieces have been fixed, acrylic paints can be used to fill and recolour areas as necessary. These should, when dry, be coated with acrylic varnish to return their wet colour.

FALLING APART

Not infrequently, quite nice pieces are found in which every joint is loose and rickety. The only thing to do with these is to knock them carefully apart and re-assemble them *in toto*.

Even loose joints are sometimes surprisingly tenacious when it comes to parting the pieces completely. A soft hammer is the tool to use here — either a rubber headed hammer or an ordinary one which has been thoroughly padded with felt and rags.

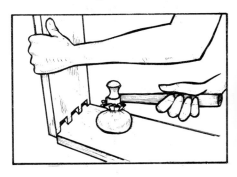

Once you have separated each piece from its neighbour, clean off all old glue and try joints dry to make sure that everything fits nicely. There is little doubt that at least some of the joints will be found to be slack and loose and, to pack these, a supply of suitable veneer is handy; where this is unobtainable in the right wood, use plywood veneers (if you are going to need a fair amount, float a piece of plywood in hot water and leave it to soak overnight to separate the veneers.)

Using plenty of glue and packing, assemble the entire piece of furniture in one go. If you do not possess enough cramps to exert pressure on all joints, tie the piece tightly together with flex or clothes line, protecting the corners of the wood with pieces of cardboard and felt.

Assuming that the piece has legs, stand it on a flat surface, making sure that all legs are in contact, while the glue dries.

FRAMING

At the highest level, framing is an art in itself. At the lowest, it is a quick method of thoroughly wrecking the appearance of a print, painting or anything else placed within it.

There is absolutely no point at all in even considering making or altering picture frames unless you have 1) the knack of visualising the appropriateness of the finished result to its picture and 2) the two essential tools: a sharp, fine saw and a good mitre guide (this **must** be made of metal and **must** be fitted with clamps to hold the moulding rock-steady while it is being cut). Extremely accurate measurement is most important, since the slight-

est error tends to appear exaggerated when the job is complete, both in ill-fitting corners and out-of-parallel sides. Due allowance must always be made for the depth of the rebate in the moulding.

The best method of marking up moulding for cutting is as follows. Measure the outside dimensions of the picture being framed (including the mount if there is one). Measure the width of your frame moulding *excluding* the rebate. Now, double the measurement of the moulding width and add this figure, plus 1/8th inch, to both height and breadth of the picture.

Take a length of moulding and, starting a little way in from one end, mark carefully (on the outside edge) the two points to be cut.

Clamp the moulding in your mitre-guide, positioning it carefully so that the saw will cut exactly through the first of your marks. Make sure that the angle of the cut will run in the right direction (i.e., it should angle inward toward the rebate).

Cut the first length of moulding and then, using this as a guide, mark the next piece for the opposite side of the frame.

When you have cut all four pieces, use the clamps on your mitre block to hold the glued corners under pressure while they dry. Evo Stik Woodworking Resin W. adhesive is as good as any for

this job.   Before the adhesive sets, drive three panel pins into each corner. These are arranged so that one goes in from the side, two from top or bottom of the frame.

The technique known as 'feathering' is a little-mentioned means of adding greatly to the strength of corners. This consists of making one or more fine saw cuts in each corner and inserting 'feathers' of veneer, whose grain must run at right angles to the mitre joint. Once inserted, these feathers are best left untrimmed until the glue has set, after which they can be pared down flush with the frame. They can be particularly effective as a feature of the design of a plain wood frame, particularly if veneer of a contrasting colour is selected for the feathers, and the added strength they give is quite phenomenal — totally disproportionate to the strength of the actual veneer.

Other methods of strengthening corners are those involving the use of dowels, metal or plywood plates and tongues.

When assembling frames, join opposite corners first to give you two L-shaped pieces which are then put together to form the completed frame.

Once the frame is fully assembled, glued and pinned, corners may be cleaned up with fine sand paper, and chips and punched-in panel pin holes filled as necessary.   Take care to

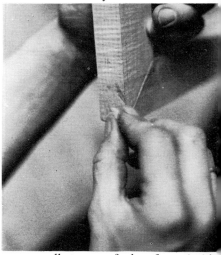

remove all traces of glue from inside the rebate — a small quantity usually squeezes out and, if left, will interfere with the corners of mount, picture and glass.

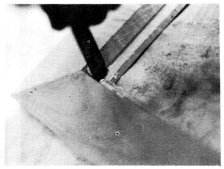

Most frames, other than those of plain wood, have a layer of gesso beneath their painted or gilded surfaces. This has been used since pre-Egyptian times as a means of preparing surfaces for painting and, although gesso can be made up to a home brew recipe, it can also be bought in tins from good artists suppliers.

The point about gesso here is that it always chips when it is sawn, no matter how carefully this is done. Since it is always gilded or painted, the small areas of damage on a newly made picture frame can be repaired with virtually anything that will take a coat of paint. Brummer — a proprietary brand of composition wood filler — is excellent for this job.

To reduce the size of an existing frame, part it at diagonally opposite corners and recut the mitres to the desired size.

Large areas of moulding that have broken away from the frame can be re-glued or, if lost, made up by taking a mould of another, identical part of the same frame and casting this in plaster of paris. For a simple design containing no undercuts, the mould can be easiest made by pressing a lump of fairly soft plasticene firmly onto the appropriate section, withdrawing it with care (withdrawal is made easier if the surface being moulded is first damped to prevent the plasticene sticking).

This is then simply filled with plaster of paris, or epoxy resin mixed with a filler of kaolin powder, and the resultant piece of moulding cut to size and glued into position.

If the moulding is more ornate and undercut, the mould will have to be made of a flexible material (also, for areas too large to mould in plasticene without it distorting as it is removed). Paribar, a compound used for dental impressions, is useful here and this has the possible advantage of being reusable many times over.

Many a humble frame has been given new status by faking an antique gold finish. This is done by first painting it red (venetian red is ideal) and then applying a good gold or bronze paint or Restoration Wax. Having applied a nice, even coat of gold, rub it carefully and unevenly from the raised areas of the frame, allowing the red to show through.

Lay the frame face down with the glass beside it. Clean the upper side of the glass thoroughly and, making sure that there are no spots or pieces of dust to be seen, lay your picture face down on it. Now lift glass and picture together to put them in the frame. You will have a piece of hardboard or card (for small frames) ready cut for the back. Lay this in and push (don't hammer) panel pins into the sides of the moulding to hold everything in place. When this has been done, seal all edges with brown paper tape. This is essential as it prevents entry of dust and insects and, to some extent, damp.

Make sure that you fit the frame

with proper eyelets of suitable strength. These should be positioned in the side-members, one third the way down from the top.

GESSO

Gesso is the traditional preparation used as a ground for painting, being applied to wood or any other surface, including canvas.

It can be bought ready made from artists' suppliers or can be made up by mixing equal quantities of glue, water, gypsum and zinc white. It is applied by painting on several thin coats, allowing each to dry before overlaying the next.

When gesso is damaged, repairs can be made with good quality plaster of paris or Brummer — a wood filler which is bought in tins from good tool shops (being a wood filler, it is obtainable in light and dark colours but, since gesso is always painted or gilded, and since Brummer can be coloured, the light is probably the more useful).

GILDING

The only two methods of gilding which concern the amateur restorer are with gold leaf or with gilding waxes. The application of gold leaf is the more expensive and difficult method, and is dealt with under its own heading.

Gilt waxes are cheaper and easier to apply than gold leaf, having the added advantage that they can be successfully used to gild a number of materials without the need for lengthy preparation of surfaces. Restoration Wax is the name of one of the better preparations and it is available from all good arts and craft shops.

Never use gold paint. It always looks like gold paint and will never blend with proper gilding, even when only used for touching up.

GLASS

Everyone has his own pet method of cleaning glass, each claiming that his is the only one for removing lime scale or wine stains or any of the other ills with which glass is beset.

First of all, try warm water, detergent and a softish brush. When this fails to remove all, an overnight soak in detergent, water and a little ammonia might be an improvement. Lime scale might yield to water to which a little spirits of salt has been added

Then there is caustic soda (no more than a five percent solution, though). I have always found (**everybody** has his favourites) that one of the following three will work on just about everything: metal polish for stains that can be rubbed at; swilling with sand or fine gravel for deposits inside bottles and decanters; and a twenty four hour soak in a bowl of water with half a dozen denture cleaning tablets for everything else. Of these three, the sand or gravel method is the most violent but, provided care is taken, no damage should result from it. (Silver sand or the fine gravel sold for fish tanks are the things to use, depending on the thickness of the deposit to be removed).

For polishing scratched glass, jeweller's rouge will sometimes have an effect but it is hard work. The principle is that glass, although hard and brittle, can be made to flow slightly. The jeweller's rouge, impregnated into a piece of chamois and applied with a fair amount of pressure, can cause this flow to take place.

Small chips round the edges of glass can be rubbed down carefully with fine emery paper, finishing with the finest of wet-or-dry paper used wet.

Glass stoppers which have become stuck in the necks of bottles or decanters should never be removed by forcible means. Try warming the bottle in the hope that the expanding air inside will help to force it out. If this doesn't work, mix up a solution of two parts alcohol to one of glycerine and one of salt, applying this liberally to the crack where stopper and bottle meet. Leave this for about twenty four hours to soak well down and try tapping the neck of the bottle (where the stopper is) gently as you turn and pull the stopper out. If neither method works alone, try both together.

Broken glass can be repaired in much the same way as broken china — Araldite being as good an adhesive as any for the purpose — but it is an unfortunate characteristic of glass that, once broken, it tends to break again near the original break.

Despite this, it is usually worthwhile making repairs and, provided a small amount of extra care is taken, there is no reason why these should not prolong the life of the piece indefinitely.

Missing pieces can be replaced by moulding them in one of the clear resins available from craft shops and a little ingenuity will solve most problems as they arise.

Perspex can be used fairly satisfactorily as a substitute for glass in certain cases and, although it scratches rather easily and tends to yellow with age, regular treatment with a metal polish will keep it bright and clean.

One obvious use for perspex is as a replacement for broken glass panels in bowed cabinets — the cost of a piece of curved glass is prohibitive in most cases (a really valuable cabinet, naturally, would justify such expense) and perspex, having a degree of flexibility makes an excellent substitute. If the curve is great, warm the perspex to allow bend-

ing but do not do this by immersing it in hot water — this sometimes turns it white and cloudy.

Should the need arise for a piece of ground or frosted glass, this can be simply made from a plain sheet. Onto a spare larger sheet or a perfectly flat piece of old slate or marble, sprinkle a quantity of carborundum powder and a little water. Laying the sheet to be ground on top of this, work it around, shifting the points at which pressure is applied. Keep plenty of powder and water between the sheets of glass and, after a while rinse and dry the piece to be used. Only when it is dry will you be able to see how far you have got. Continue the process until the frosting is evenly applied to the entire area.

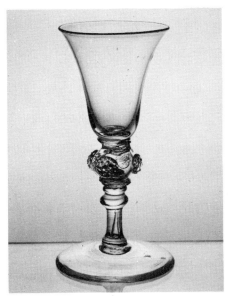

An unusual 18th century coin glass containing a George III threepenny piece dated 1762. Modern adhesives bring the repair of glass into the scope of the amateur restorer.

GOLD

Gold is a widely used, and widely faked, metal. One of the simplest tests for purity is to wash a tarnished piece in soap and water — if it remains tarnished, the gold has been alloyed with other metals in which case an ammonia solution should clean it adequately.

Rather better tests involve the use of acids: a fifty percent solution of nitric acid will turn gold green if it is less than nine carats.

Aqua Regia (three parts hydrochloric acid added to one of nitric) will turn the gold a paler colour if it is less than eighteen carats.

GOLD LEAF AND INLAY

Working with gold leaf is tricky and exasperating, but well worthwhile from the points of view of both personal satisfaction and the increased value of the article concerned.

A good gesso base is essential and this should be carefully rubbed down to a perfectly smooth surface.

As always, the article to be treated must be perfectly clean — having removed all obvious dirt, wipe over with a cotton wool swab moistened with a weak ammonia solution — and gold leaf is best applied in a warm, dust free atmosphere.

Once the base has been prepared, and the ammonia solution has dried completely, a coat of gold size is applied.

When this has become almost dry and barely tacky, the gold leaf is laid on in sheets using a camel hair brush to help lift and smooth the sheets into position.

Sheets of gold leaf should be applied so that they overlap slightly — all in the same direction, like roofing tiles — small gaps being filled with odd pieces.

If the gold size is too tacky, the leaves will tend to wrinkle; if it is too dry, they will fail to adhere properly.

When the area being treated is completely covered, rub it gently with the softest of cotton cloths, always in the direction of the overlapping leaves so as not to lift off the work.

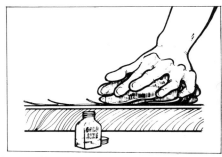

Finally, coat the area with size or varnish.

While this method is fine for picture frames and irregular surfaces, flat areas are more likely to be gilded successfully if the coat of size is allowed to dry thoroughly and the leaves of gold floated on with a little water.

When dry, the job is varnished or sized as before.

A quicker, easier method of producing a gilded effect is to use Reeves' Restoration Wax or Windsor and Newton's Treasure Wax (either of which is obtainable through artists' suppliers) which are made in several colours and shades and which are simply rubbed onto the smooth surface with a finger and buffed up to a good lustre.

HEAT MARKS

Heat marks usually show as white, cloudy rings on the surfaces of tables, indicating where cups of tea, hot dishes and plates have been placed without the use of saucers or table mats.

Although their presence calls forth cries of despair from elderly relatives, they are usually not too difficult to remove being related to the white water marks dealt with under **Bleaching.**

Their presence indicates that moisture has penetrated into the polish and they are removed by firm rubbing with the finest wire wool (000 grade) dipped in oil. Even this may not be necessary: a mixture of equal quantities of linseed oil and turps applied to the mark and left to soak for an hour or two might do the trick.

The first thing to try, however, is to moisten a finger with a little linseed oil and rub the mark hard — until the heat generated becomes painful. Only if this fails need other remedies be employed.

HINGES

There are only four things that can go wrong with hinges; they can seize up solid with a build up of rust, they can snap (particularly the cast iron butts used for heavy work), their central pins can wear through and break, and their screws can pull out of the wood, tearing it and making it too weak to allow replacement screws to bite and hold.

Hinges that have seized up are best dosed liberally with penetrating oil and left for a day or two, after which they can be tapped gently with a hammer and gradually worked until they open (or close). If they are badly pitted and look as though they will soon give way, they can then be replaced.

Snapped hinges must obviously be replaced.

When central pins wear through, these can be replaced with panel pins or nails of a suitable gauge. Using a nail punch or a nail, tap out the old pin and replace it with a panel pin or nail which has been cut to the correct length with a hacksaw or wire cutter. The heads of nails will need to be filed down somewhat, but they should be left larger than the diameter of the nails in order that they do not fall through the hinge.

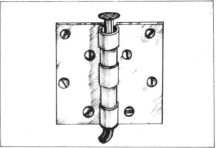

The worst fault of hinges is that, through constant use and too much strain, their screws are sometimes pulled from the woodwork causing considerable damage. Although temporary repairs can usually be effected by means of matchsticks glued into the holes and the use of longer screws, sooner or later a new piece of wood will have to be spliced into the frame.

A piece of wood of the right type and colour is dovetailed into position and polished to match the rest of the piece.

The old wood is cut away with saw and chisel.

The new piece is glued and cramped in position.

When the glue has set, the new

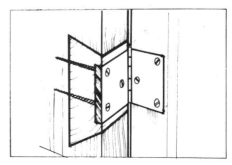

piece is rubbed down to the level of the surrounding wood.

Finally, after staining and polishing, the hinges are screwed back with screws that ideally pass through the new wood into the old.

HORN

Objects made of horn have often been shaped by first being softened in hot water. For this reason, it is inadvisable to soak dirty horn in hot water, since warping can result. Wash it in warm, soapy water and dry it immediately with a soft cloth.

Powder and drinking horns are not infrequently etched with patterns or scenes, the lines being made more distinct by means of having colour rubbed into them. Where this requires brightening, it can be done with indian ink or black boot polish (the latter only on grey—black horns). Dull horn responds well to metal polish and can be finished with a light wax polish.

Repairs are best made with cellulose adhesive, and impregnation with polyvinyl acetate will prevent flaking — an ill to which horn easily falls prey.

Loose metal mounts and fittings can be fixed either with epoxy resin adhesive or, if rivetted, by means of small rivets of the appropriate material.

IRON

When iron is badly rusted, little or nothing can be done for it but, for the rust to have reached these proportions, the metal must have been neglected for many, many years.

Large areas can usually be safely attacked with a wire brush to remove most of the rust and then, to finish off, fine emery cloth used with a little

oil will bring the surface up brightly. After removing the oil with a suitable solvent (such as petrol) iron should always be treated to prevent moisture and air from reaching its surface. Clear varnish, thin oil, Vaseline or black boot polish are best for objects requiring a bright finish — black paint of one kind or another is usually used for all others, particularly those of cast iron.

Cast iron looks strong but is inclined to be brittle. Once it has snapped, there is little that can be done since it is extremely difficult to weld. Sometimes a break can be repaired by careful drilling and bolting flat steel splints onto each side of the broken member, but

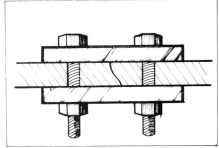

this is rather unsightly. Epoxy resin adhesives are moderately successful.

Holes can be filled effectively by wetting iron filings and packing them together (ask for iron cement at a builders' merchant or large ironmonger). The result is a hard piece of iron which can be filed to shape — holes and

cracks are filled by packing them with iron cement and filing away the surplus after it has set.

Iron powder filler can be bought for use with fibreglass resins and some use may be made of this to cast decorative features.

IVORY

Generally speaking, the cleaning and preserving techniques for ivory are the same as those for bone (q.v.).

Because of its greater value, and because it is used for much finer work, ivory should, perhaps, be treated a little more carefully than bone in that advice should be sought from an expert on the subject when there is occasion for doubt about the state of preservation of the material.

Unlike bone, ivory is formed of a series of laminations which, because of age or bad storage conditions, can separate. Impregnation with wax is the recommended treatment for old ivory in poor condition but, once again, specialist advice should be sought if there is any doubt.

Carved ivory (indeed, all ivory) which has not been exposed to light tends to go yellow. While this colour is a disadvantage in the case of piano keys or knife handles, it is often found to enhance the value of carved pieces and chessmen. To bleach those objects which would benefit from the treatment, mix whiting with twenty volume hydrogen peroxide to make a stiff paste. Smear this onto the ivory and stand it in the sunshine to dry.

When the paste has dried, a damp cloth may be used to wipe it off after which, the ivory should be carefully and thoroughly dried. **Never immerse ivory in water to wash it**. This can

A 19th century Japanese ivory (King & Chasemore).

sometimes cause the laminations to open and frequent or prolonged soaking can cause irreparable damage.

An occasional wipe over with cotton wool just moistened with almond oil will help to keep ivory in good condition.

Repairs can be carried out using white shellac as an adhesive. The more adventurous will wish to attempt the

really workmanlike method which entails dowelling broken pieces together with small ivory pins. Missing parts should be carved from ivory if they are to be at all worthwhile for, moulded replacements are never satisfactory.

JADE

There are three different types, of jade — jadeite, nephrite and 'Siberian Jade' — and all are extremely hard. Hard enough to scratch glass.

Cleaning is best carried out with soap and water — fine detail being strong enough to stand up to light scrubbing with a softish nylon or bristle brush.

Refix broken pieces with Araldite or a polyvinyl acetate adhesive, being sure to apply pressure during the curing time.

Chips and missing pieces can be filled with appropriately-coloured wax, sealing wax or coloured synthetic resin, and polished, when set, with metal polish.

JAPANNING

The term japanning is used in a very wide context. Originally, it was applied to any Oriental painted decoration but later its meaning was extended to include any highly polished opaque finish.

Japanned finishes are extremely fragile owing to the brittle nature of the medium used — a lacquer made from asphaltum, resin, turpentine and linseed oil — and are usually found to have been employed over gesso.

The usual damage sustained by japanned finishes is flaking caused by damp penetrating the support. Chipping caused by even quite gentle knocks is another source of annoyance.

The usual method of repair is to colour the damaged area with paint to match the surrounding shade, and build up the thickness with several coats of high gloss varnish.

JET

Jet is a kind of bituminous coal which was widely used for jewellery during the nineteenth century, as well as for small items such as thimble cases and paper knives. It takes a high polish, for which reason black glass has been widely used as a substitute, but glass is heavier than jet, size for size, and is easily detectable.

Clean jet by rubbing with fresh breadcrumbs or wiping with a piece of cotton-wool moistened with soapy water. Repair with epoxy resin and fill chips with black sealing wax or resin with a ciment fondu filler.

JEWELLERY

There is really very little that can be done to repair broken jewellery by anyone but a professional jeweller. Cheaper stones may be refixed in their settings with spots of epoxy resin adhesive carefully applied, and beads can be re-strung with little trouble. But valuable pieces and more complicated repairs should always be left to the experts.

When re-stringing beads, silk or terylene thread is best, and it should be carefully knotted between each bead in order to prevent loss at such time that it may break.

For cleaning individual pieces seek the advice of a jeweller. See also 'Gold' or 'Silver' headings.

Perhaps more important than repairs to jewellery is the proper care of pieces. Naturally, harder, sharp faceted stones should always be kept apart from pearls and other easily scratched surfaces. Ideally each piece should be individually boxed but, where this is not possible, a well-designed jewel box with plenty of separate compartments should be used.

Most jewellery too, benefits from being worn regularly — particularly pearls.

JOINTS WITH ADHESIVES

Repairs to individual joints are described under their various headings. General rules, however, apply to all jointing and joining of materials.

Parts to be joined must always be absolutely clean and free from grease — just touching a surface with your hand is enough to prevent some adhesives from bonding some materials properly.

To aid adhesion, surfaces to be joined should not be perfectly smooth. When the break has left smooth surfaces — as in the case of glass — these should be gently abraded before gluing.

Contrary to much popular opinion, the best joins are not made by sandwiching a good thick layer of strong adhesive between the broken pieces. The only satisfactory joins are made by applying pressure to the pieces being joined; this squeezes out all but the thinnest coat of glue and brings the two surfaces as nearly into direct contact with each other as possible.

Undue haste is always to be avoided. Adhesives need varying lengths of time to set properly and these are always given in the manufacturer's instructions. Releasing pressure or applying strain to repaired pieces before this time is up can do nothing but weaken the join. Squeezed-out glue may well have dried long before the recommended time is up but remember that this has been exposed to the air while the glue actually doing the job has not.

LACE

Lace was usually made with cotton or linen thread — sometimes silk — and is always very delicate, requiring extreme care in handling.

As always, cleaning should be carried out before any repairs are attempted. This should be done carefully by hand — NEVER in a washing-machine!

Because the weight of water held in any fabric being washed is considerable, even moderately sized pieces of lace should be tacked to a piece of muslin before immersion. Large pieces can be folded in two or four before being backed.

Where possible valuable lace should be soaked in two or three changes of distilled water, the last containing a few pure soap flakes, and rinsed finally in distilled water. Never rub or wring lace, move it in the water and, at most, squeeze it very gently to remove stubborn dirt. To dry, stretch the lace gently flat on clean blotting paper or several layers of clean white sheeting. Shape can be preserved by pinning the lace, working from the centre outwards, with stainless pins when it is laid to dry.

This can be an extremely tedious task requiring, possibly, hundreds of pins since it is sometimes necessary to pin almost every hole in the lace.

If, for any reason, lace cannot be washed, lay it flat and sprinkle liberally with white talcum powder (french chalk) then brush it off with a soft paintbrush.

Repair methods will depend to some extent on the way in which the particular piece of lace was made, the kind of damage and the intricacy of the designs. A little ingenuity with a fine needle and thread will overcome most problems. Take care, though, to match the colour of new thread carefully to that of the old before repairs are undertaken. A quick dip in tea will age the appearance of new cotton quite effectively.

LACQUER

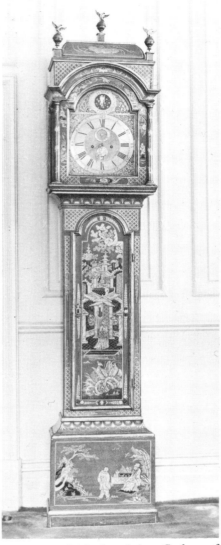

Longcase clock by John Crolee of Lincoln, with a fine red lacquered case.

The best of lacquer work comes exclusively from either China or Japan, though a considerable amount has been produced in Britain, particularly during the nineteenth century.

Work is built up of a number of coats of pigmented resin from the Rhus Vernicifera tree and then carved or painted, sometimes very beautifully. To clean and polish lacquer work, use a paste of flour and olive oil, applying this with a soft cloth before polishing with silk. **Never use spirits or other solvents.**

Owing to the brittle nature of lacquer, it is frequently found to be in need of repair. Plaster of paris or most other modelling materials will doubtless prove equally satisfactory for the purpose, matching being effected by means of 'lacquer' paints.

LEAD

Lead is rarely used structurally or decoratively in its own right, though some garden ornaments such as statuettes and flower tubs may be found of this material.

Newly melted lead is a bright silvery colour which dulls quite soon to the familiar grey. As the metal ages further, it develops a whitish coating — carbonate of lead — which is normally left uncleaned.

Dents, of course, can usually be pushed out (or hammered gently, preferably with a wooden or hard rubber hammer) owing to the softness of the metal, but repairs to lead are made difficult by the metal's extremely low melting point. Holes and cracks can sometimes be hammered together, otherwise an epoxy resin with a lead filler could be used. The latter is not particularly successful, since it is difficult to match the colour of old lead which, since it is left uncleaned, continues to change.

LEATHER

Being strong, decorative, flexible and readily available, leather has natural-ly been used for a great many purposes for a great many years. Unfortunately, leather tends to deteriorate badly if not kept properly, and many leather-covered objects will be found to be in such a sorry state that there is no alter-native to recovering them if they are to be granted extensions to their lives.

Badly stained and dirty leather can often be improved by washing with soap and water (pure soap, not detergent) or rubbing gently with petrol or white spirit. Always test carefully for colour fastness before sailing into important pieces.

To Inset or Replace Leather on Desk and Table Tops.

When there is no alternative to replacing the old leather, first remove this and all traces of glue from the wood beneath. Remember that any and every irregularity in the wood surface will show through the leather covering and may even be exaggerated by it.

Generally speaking, the leather will be found to have been surrounded by a strip of veneer as a means of adjust-ing the comparitive levels of the surfaces of the leather and the edge area of the table top. Great care must be taken with the cleaning at this point, if the new leather is not to rise above the level of the veneer, the wood beneath must be perfectly clean but the edge of the veneer must not be damaged in any way or the final job will have unsightly joins.

Cut a piece of leather slightly larger than the area to be covered — about ½" all round will do — and coat both the leather and the wood surface with glue — Polycel is perfectly adequate for this.

Smooth the leather gently down with a soft cloth pad, working from the centre to drive out air bubbles. Do not press too hard or the leather will tend to stretch, probably unevenly.

When the adhesive is almost dry, mark the leather with a blunt point such as a knitting needle, thumbnail or other, handy implement along the edge of the veneer. This can be done quite adequately by feel.

Using a long straightedge, prefer-ably of metal, cut the leather carefully along the mark, angling the knife slightly so that the leather is undercut.

Work round the edge of the leather, pressing it firmly down all round.

When the work is perfectly dry, it can be tooled using one of the wheels of various patterns obtainable from art and craft suppliers.

The line to be followed is lightly marked on the leather surface and the tooling wheel cleaned with meths and heated to a temperature below that at which it would scorch the leather. Draw the wheel round the line marked, apply-ing sufficient pressure to indent its pat-tern clearly onto the surface.

Gold can be applied to the tooling by means of the spools of gold tape transfer which, again, can be bought at art and craft shops.

A final treatment with the British Museum Leather Dressing will start the new leather top on the road to long life and good looks.

It is possible to improve the appearance of a wooden topped desk whose veneer is in bad condition by insetting a piece of leather where there was none before.

With a sharp knife, score a line round the surface to be covered. This incision should be between one sixteenth and one eighth of an inch deep.

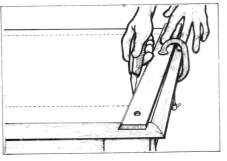

Chamfer the surface of the desk to meet the cut.

Clean all polish and dirt from the area to be covered — a scraper will remove most, and this can be followed by a suitable solvent and sandpaper.

Continue as with a replacement

piece of leather, pressing the trimmed edges well into the chamfer.

All leather will benefit from regular treatment of some kind and the following are recommended; Vaseline, castor oil, lanoline or sperm oil. Neat's foot oil is not thought to be of much value.

To improve absorption, any of these oils should be warmed slightly before application with a soft cloth.

LEGS

The cures for broken legs on furniture (as on humans) are much the same as those for broken arms.

Splits in the wood are best glued and cramped or, if this is impractical, new pieces should be spliced in.

If the joints have become loose, the leg will have to be removed, cleaned and glued back into place. This may prove a somewhat longer job than that presented by a loose arm.

Because of the way chair legs are jointed to the top rails, it is usually necessary to remove the front or back rail entirely. A sharp couple of taps with a padded hammer is usually sufficient to do this.

Once the rail with its pair of legs is off, the loose leg may be removed easily and all joints carefully cleaned. Reassembling is best done in one go, pressure being applied to all joints while the glue sets.

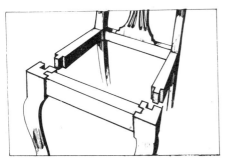

If the member concerned is a table leg, it will usually be necessary to remove the table top before actual repair operations commence. This is normally held in place by means of a few screws through the upper rail of the frame.

It may sometimes be considered advisable to glue a triangular block behind the leg as a means of providing extra strength to the repair.

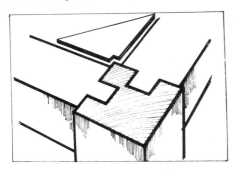

LOCKS

One of the great aggravations in life is a piece of furniture containing locked drawers or cupboards whose keys are missing.

The very last method of opening locked drawers and cupboards is to force them with a levering, prising or bashing tool.

Always try every available key of approximately the right size — most furniture locks are pretty simple affairs and most, too, are fairly similar. It is a good idea to keep all small keys for just such an eventuality.

Locks fitted to drawers can usually be unscrewed from the inside. If possible, remove the drawer immediately -above. If there are dust boards between the drawers, one of these will also have to be removed to allow access to the rear of the lock.

It may not be possible to unscrew the lock from above. If not, the dust boards from the back of the piece will have to come off to allow access from the back.

If neither of these manoeuvres allow the job to be done, it may be necessary to remove the back of the drawer itself.

If the drawer is a long one, or if it is impractical to work from the back of the piece of furniture, the rail above the drawer into which the bolt of the lock fits may often be bent upward sufficiently far to allow the bolt to clear its socket.

This is best done with a screw clamp but care must be taken or the rail is likely to break.

If all else fails, place a punch on the lock pin and hit it smartly with a hammer. This should drive the lock back into the drawer, pulling the screws from the wood. With luck, it will only be the inside of the drawer that suffers damage.

In the unlikely event that even this treatment fails, chisel away the rail above the lock, and having obtained a key (or having fitted a new lock to which you have a key), splice a piece of wood into the rail to make as invisible a repair as possible.

Locked doors present similar problems to locked drawers and the remedies are equally similar. Added difficulty is sometimes caused here, however, owing to the fact that many cupboard doors will be glazed and too much bending will crack the glass.

Double doors are sometimes a little easier to open. Prise up the top rail and locate the bolt. Having found it, this can usually be coaxed out of the way with a knife blade and the doors pulled open until the lock frees itself.

MARBLE

A good scrub with soap and water is the best cleansing treatment for most white marble — some coloured marbles can suffer a little harm from this and should be experimented with before launching a full scale attack, particularly in the case of valuable carved pieces.

A strong cleaner for run-of-the mill pieces of marble is a mixture of equal amounts by volume of caustic potash, quicklime, soap and water. The soap is shaved into the water and boiled gently until completely dissolved. Potash and quicklime are then added and the mixture is brushed onto the marble and left for a few days before being washed off.

Stains can be treated safely with petrol, benzine, alcohol and acetone, but care should be taken always to use white, and not coloured, cloths. Since marble is polished with wax, these treatments are going to remove not only the stains but the polish too. This is likely to be more distressing on old marble than new, because marble acquires an age patination.

Being relatively soft, marble can be rubbed down with abrasives and files if necessary to remove unsightly chips — this, naturally, should only be

done with wash stand tops and other, unimportant pieces.

As good a polish as any for white marble is wet chalk, which is simply rubbed over the surface and followed by buffing with a soft cloth. Silicone wax rubbed well in will help to preserve the surface and is particularly to be recommended for outside statuary.

MARQUETRY

Owing to the effects of time and central heating on old glues, marquetry work will sometimes be found to be lifting and cockling. Repair involves removing all loose or badly fixed pieces and re-glueing or replacing them.

A damp cloth and hot iron should be used to lift badly glued pieces. For larger areas, a household iron, for individual pieces, a soldering iron should be used. The idea is to create steam and force it into the glue to soften it; polish is liable to inhibit this action and should be removed before operations commence.

Base wood and the reverse side of the pieces of veneer should be thoroughly cleaned before they are stuck back into place. If a piece is missing, all other pieces should be stuck down and then a pattern made of the missing piece. This is done in the same way that a brass rubbing is made; a piece of paper

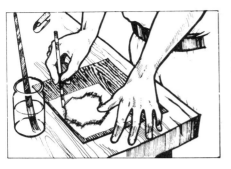

Paste this lightly onto a piece of suitable veneer and cut round the outline with a scalpel or single edged razor blade, cutting both pattern and veneer in one go.

Glue the piece into place, lay a sheet of wax paper over the area and apply pressure — either weights or a piece of wood cramped down over it.

A quicker repair for missing pieces is simply to drop wax or shellac, suitably coloured, into the space and rub it down to match the surrounding level when it has cooled.

is laid over the area and rubbed with a soft pencil to obtain an outline.

Marquetry work at its finest — a late 18th century Dutch marquetry cylinder bureau. (King & Chasemore).

A very rare, William III mirror worth over £5,000. Definitely not to be tampered with, as even professional re-silvering would reduce its value dramatically. (Sotheby & Co.)

MIRRORS

The resilvering of mirrors is a job for professionals. It can, however, be attempted at home and, with practice, a reasonably good job can be done.

First, remove all old silver and paint with nitric acid — taking great care not to splash skin, eyes or clothes in the process. Wash the glass thoroughly with detergent and plenty of warm water. From this point on, do not touch the surface of the glass with anything not mentioned below. The glass should now be coated with stannous chloride and rinsed.

A solution of silver nitrate and sodium potassium tartrate is now prepared and applied to the dry glass with brush or spray gun.

When this has dried, apply a coat of shellac varnish to seal it and follow this with a coat of paint.

Blemishes in the finish will be due to fingermarks or grease on the glass.

This treatment can be applied to small areas of damage without stripping the mirror completely but great care must be taken with the cleaning, or the new and old silvering will not blend.

Never resilver old mirrors, as this will considerably reduce their value

MOTHER OF PEARL

Mother of pearl is a very soft substance and chipped pieces can be improved by rubbing with a fine file before polishing with jeweller's rouge.

Since there is no suitable substitute, missing pieces have to be replaced. This is not too difficult, since the material can be easily cut with a fret saw, filed to shape and stuck down with shellac or almost any other adhesive. Mother of pearl inlay work was made by sticking on the mother of pearl and

Typical 19th century mother-of-pearl inlay work from the top of a papier mache workbox.

building up the interstices with black varnish — missing varnish can be easiest replaced with black wax.

MOUNTS

Almost all prints, drawings and watercolours are attached in one way or another to a cardboard mount. This is frequently damaged, dirty, or both. Unless the mount has a particular value of some kind the best course is usually to remove the old mount and replace it with a clean, new one.

Pictures are normally fixed to their mounts with paper tape or simple flour- or gelatine-based adhesives. All of these may be removed by carefully moistening the paper or mount and waiting for the adhesive to soften.

By far the most attractive, and professional looking, mounts for the majority of subjects are those of the cut-out variety. A great deal of unnecessary mystique attaches to the proper cutting of these mounts — and it really is quite a simple job which demands nothing more than a very sharp craft knife, a metal straightedge and a certain amount of care.

Having selected a suitable piece

of card, measure carefully the area of picture which you wish to display and the size of the frame into which it will fit.

Cut the card to fit the frame.

Now mark the rectangle to be cut out. Since a picture is usually mounted in such a way that the sides and top of the mount are of roughly equal widths, and slightly narrower than the bottom, a little calculation might be necessary to ensure that the rectangle is correctly placed. As good a method as any is to cut a piece of paper or card 1/8 of an inch larger each way than the size you wish the aperture to be, and place this on the mount in the correct position, drawing lightly round it in pencil.

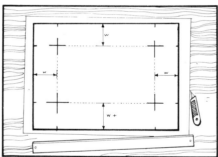

Remember that the aperture you are to cut will have an angled edge which must be allowed for — the extra 1/8th inch on your measurements does this.

Having marked the rectangle, put a new, stout blade in your craft knife (Stanley knives are among the best for this purpose, since the blades are fairly inflexible).

Lay the mount on a piece of old card (this should be free from ridges and old score-marks) and place your metal straightedge in position for the first cut. The safest method here is to position the straightedge *inside* the aperture marking.

Now, angling the knife at about 45 degrees, make your first cut. Considerable pressure is required on both straightedge and knife because the cut must be clean. If you have to go over it again, you are almost certain to spoil the look of the mount. The knife must enter the mount exactly at the corner of the aperture and its cut must end, too, at exactly the right place.

Work round the card, making all four cuts in order. When the fourth cut has been made, the unwanted centre of the mount should lift out. Possibly it will still be held by the corners. Provided you have done your cutting well, it can be pushed out gently without causing any damage.

When you have removed the unwanted piece of card, look carefully at the corners of the aperture. If they contain any fluffy fragments these can be easily cut away.

Some pictures look best in plain mounts, others benefit from a pattern of wash lines drawn round the aperture.

To draw these you will need a lining pen, a child's paint box and a good quality watercolour brush.

First, work out the arrangement of lines you intend to draw, marking the edge of a small piece of paper or card correspondingly (this is much quicker than measuring them all out with a ruler). Use this to mark the mount lightly with a soft pencil, drawing in the lines where they intersect to make corners.

With a pin, carefully prick the position of each drawn corner on the mount and erase the pencil marks

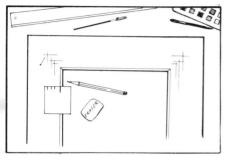

Mix up a light wash of suitable colour from your pencil paint box — using water, not white paint, to make the colour lighter. Make plenty of wash. If you run out halfway through the job you will probably be unable to match the colours.

To ensure clean work, it is important for right-handed people to have the colour wash on their right as they work. This helps to prevent accidental blots.

Now, lay the straight-edge in position for one of the inside lines and charge the lining-pen by filling your paint brush with wash and wiping it over the pen.

Make a test line on another piece of card and, if it is alright for colour, immediately draw your first line. Speed here is essential, because, if left, the pigments in the wash will tend to separate from the water, causing the line to be dark at the beginning and lighter at the end.

Work round the mount clockwise, until all the lines are drawn. Charge

the pen freshly immediately before drawing each line.

Leave to dry before washing-in any broader bands of colour.

When the lines are dry, broad bands may be washed in carefully between any pair.

Charge your brush with wash (test the colour first by applying some to a similar piece of card and leaving it to dry) and draw it out smoothly along one side of the mount, being careful not to overlap the lines already drawn. As soon as you reach the end of the first side, rinse the brush and quickly squeeze it dry, using it to soak up all surplus wash from the mount. Repeat all round the mount.

The easy way to fix the picture to the mount is this: onto the rear side of the upper edge of the picture, stick two small pieces of brown paper tape, wetting them well and allowing them to protrude above the paper.

Lay the picture, face uppermost, on a flat surface and then carefully lay the mount over it in the correct position. Press firmly on the mount at the points where the sticky tape is.

Lift the mount carefully — the picture should be hanging down the back of it — and turn it over. Now run a single strip of sticky tape right along the top edge of the picture

Do not stick the sides or bottom. This can cause the picture to buckle or even tear as, over the years, it expands and contracts with moisture or dryness.

Some other objects, (silhouettes, cameos, etc.) show to advantage in an oval mount.

Although it is possible to cut a chamfered oval mount by hand, this is rather tricky since, unless you have a metal oval of the correct size, it would have to be done freehand.

Far easier is to cover the mount with velvet, silk or other material.

To draw the oval: lay the card on a flat surface and push in two pins (panel pins driven through the card into a piece of wood underneath might be better). Now cut a piece of thin string a little longer than twice the distance between the pins, tying the ends securely together. Lay the string on the card so that it's circumference encloses the pins.

With a sharp pencil, pushing outward against the string, draw your oval. A few trials may be necessary to establish the correct length of string and the spacing of the pins. The less slack there is in the string, the longer will be the oval.

Assuming you intend covering the mount with material, cut out the oval as accurately as possible, using a sharp craft knife. Irregularities in the shape may be smoothed with glasspaper after it is cut.

Coat one side of the card with adhesive (Copydex or Polycell are best) and lay over it a piece of material, preferably to overlap by half an inch all round.

Working by feel, cut a slit in the material the full length of the oval. Now make a number of radial cuts from centre to edge of the oval. The number needed will vary with the shape of the oval (the sharper the curves the more cuts needed). Having made your cuts, turn the mount over and apply glue to the back, bringing the loose material through the middle and smoothing it down onto the adhesive Glue the back edges of the mount and turn the edges of the material over cutting off the corners of the material to avoid bulges.

MOUNTANTS

The best mountants for paper are those employing gum arabic a the adhesive ingredient. As good a recipe as any requires four ounces of gum arabic to one of glycerine and twelve of water. This is mixed by dissolving the gum arabic in boiling water and adding the glycerine, stirring thoroughly. In these instant times however, with so many proprietary glues and pastes on the market, few people will feel it worthwhile to make their own.

It is, however, important to be

sure that adhesives used for prints, drawings, watercolours and other paper or delicate objects contain nothing that will harm them: They must be colourless to avoid risk of unsightly and damaging stains, and should always be easily soluble in water or other innocuous substance.

It is almost never necessary to mount any delicate substance by coating its surface with adhesive. Always, therefore, use the minimum amount of adhesive or sticky tape, applying it only along the extreme upper edge.

MUSICAL BOXES

Although there are a few snuff boxes to be found containing musical movements, these are so intricate that only skilled restorers should ever be permitted to tinker with them. Far more common are the relatively large musical boxes in wooden cases.

Generally, there is little beyond cleaning that the amateur can do to improve the working of a musical box and, since any mechanical damage is liable to be permanent, repairs to moving parts are best left to skilled hands.

One of the cardinal rules regarding the care of musical boxes is never to leave a tune unfinished. If the movement runs down before the end of a tune, give a few winds to the handle and, as soon as the tune has ended, stop the motor. This ensures that no pins are in contact with the comb. Should the box be picked up or tilted with pins and comb still in contact, it is quite likely that the cylinder would move on its spindle sufficiently to break or damage the comb or the pins.

If, for any reason, the cylinder should run unchecked by the speed regulating mechanism, lasting damage is sure to be sustained by either the comb or the pins. Before working on motor, cylinder or any other moving parts, therefore, always ensure that the spring is unwound and always remove the comb. These are vitally important precautions.

Sometimes the comb will be found to be rusty. Resist the temptation to attack with a file or emery cloth. Instead, remove the comb carefully from the box and scrub the teeth gently with a brass wire brush, perhaps with a little light oil. Never brush across the teeth, always along them.

To clean a dirty cylinder, first remove the comb. Rotate the cylinder slowly, washing away greasy dirt with benzene applied on a soft toothbrush or nail brush. Liquid metal polish can be applied and brushed off with a toothbrush — do not use a rag, as this will catch on the pins and could cause damage.

A 19th century musical box equipped with three six inch cylinders. Never stop a musical box with a tune unfinished. (King & Chasemore)

NEEDLEWORK

The great problem arising out of cleaning old needlework of any kind is that of colour fastness. Check this by placing a piece of white blotting paper under the work and damping a small area above it. Every colour used in the work should be tested in this way before any attempt is made to wash it.

Assuming that the colours are fast, the article may be carefully washed in lukewarm water to which a gentle liquid detergent or pure soap has been added.

If colour fastness is in doubt, immerse the material carefully in a dish of carbon tetrachloride or turpentine substitute. Do this only in a well ventilated room.

Always dry these materials flat in a warm place.

A safer method of cleaning, particularly for delicate materials and those whose colours are not fast, is to coat them with warm, dry potato flour and then brush this off again with a soft brush such as a household paint brush or one of the kind sold for babies' hair.

Tapestries to be rehung will benefit from being backed by a piece of nylon or terylene net material which can be sewn on and which will help take the strain imposed by the weight of the tapestry on the areas around the rings.

ONYX

Onyx, and, indeed, most other decorative stones are best repaired with Araldite, though none of the resin preparations will easily take a high gloss finish.

If there are chips missing, it is possible to replace these with suitably coloured Araldite, or sometimes with wax.

Wax repairs will, of course be much simpler but less durable than those employing Araldite, and they are often used as a means of tarting up a piece for display purposes.

The difficulty of producing a glossy finish on epoxy resins can be overcome to a certain extent by mixing up a quantity of material of the right colour and then pouring it onto a sheet of glass which has first been carefully coated with a parting agent. By this means, the resin will take a reasonably good finish from the glass. Once the resin has cured, it can be removed from the glass and worked with a file to produce fragments of the right size and shape to fit into the spaces left by the missing pieces of onyx.

This is a fiddly, tricky business and is best experimented with before full-scale restorations are undertaken.

ORMOLU

To clean ordinary ormolu castings, first remove them from the article and then scrub them with soapy water to which a little ammonia has been added. Always rinse them well with fresh water after cleaning, and dry them thoroughly, either with a cloth or in warm air.

If the ormolu has been gilded, naturally more care must be taken and, although the treatment is basically the same, use only a soft brush, wiping, rather than scrubbing, the surface gold. As soon as the gilt is clean, rinse and dry carefully, preferably in a warm stream of air — a hair dryer or fan heater turned low would be ideal.

If the gilding is in need of restoration, gold leaf can be applied (see appropriate heading) but there are easier ways.

For relatively smooth, uncomplicated pieces, good old Restoration Wax

Louis XV gaming machine with fine ormolu mounts. (Sotheby & Co.)

works well but, since this is applied with a finger, it often fails to penetrate the crevices which are found on the more elaborate ormolu castings. For these, there is a liquid, gold leaf paint which can be bought from art and craft suppliers and this is applied with a brush. When the liquid leaf has dried, it should be given a coat of fixative to protect it.

It will sometimes be found that ormolu decoration, has been lacquered and this has worn off in patches. Before cleaning, all lacquer should be removed with acetone.

PACKING

The packing of valuable and delicate objects is a specialised field in itself, and one in which it is impossible to take too much care. Where large pieces, a great many different pieces, or even a single piece of great value, are involved, it would be foolhardy not to call in experts from a firm of proven reliability.

The purpose of packing is to preserve an object from harm of all kinds, usually during transportation. This does not simply involve wrapping it in newspaper and hoping for the best. Care must be taken to ensure that the piece will arrive not only unbroken, but free from the effects of damp, heat, and the attentions of insects and thieves.

As a general rule, each object should be contained in its own stout carton or crate, strong enough to withstand severe knocks and the pressure of other objects being piled on top. It should be securely held in its container in such a way that it can never bang or rub against the inside. Whenever possible, all projecting ornaments and other pieces should be removed and packed separately in the same container. Where this is not possible, they should receive special protection against damage.

Loose shelves should be removed from furniture, tied or taped together and packed safely in the same container in such a way that there is no risk of them moving and damaging either themselves or the main piece.

Corners should always receive special attention, as should delicate legs and stretchers. Drawers are best locked, their keys taped or tied securely to a convenient part of the piece. Unlockable drawers should be tied in, the corners of the piece being padded to prevent chaffing.

Pictures in frames are best packed, well padded, in individual wooden boxes. If the frames are glazed, the glass is best removed and packed between sheets of ply or hardboard behind the frame so that, even if it does break, no damage will be sustained by the picture.

All packing materials should be clean, dry and free from insects, particular attention being paid to straw, wood shavings and rags. It is rarely a good idea to wrap pieces directly in polythene: changes in temperature can easily cause condensation to form inside the polythene and veneered objects, for instance, could well sustain considerable damage.

As a final precaution, no matter how well the packing has been done, or by whom, make sure that all pieces are adequately insured against all possible eventualities. Any reputable Insurance Broker will happily advise.

PAINT (removal of, from pores and end-grain).

There is no quick and easy method of removing old paint from the pores of wood — either the large, open pores of oak, walnut, mahogany or any other of the large-pored woods, or the end grain of any other woods.

First try scrubbing paint remover right into the pores with a stiff-bristled brush. With luck, this will remove the paint from the openings of the pores to a sufficient depth to allow dry colour to be rubbed in to conceal the unwanted tint. Failing this, the wood will have to be scraped, sanded, planed or sawn back past the penetration level of the paint.

PAPIER MACHE

The best repairs to papier mache are made with papier mache.

Shred newspaper, brown paper or any other coarse grained paper into water and leave it to soak for twenty-four hours — if the water is hot it helps — then drain off the excess water and add some polycell or flour paste, stirring the resulting mess well.

To repair papier mache objects, simply press pieces of the mixture into place, squeezing out as much moisture as possible, and leave to dry. Once the papier mache has dried, it will be hard and strong and can be worked with saw, coarse file or sandpaper.

To fill holes in a hurry, particularly if they are to be painted over, use plastic wood, Brummer, or any other quick drying filling compound.

Victorian Papier Mache furniture. (King & Chasemore)

Three early Georgian pewter flagons whose patina needs only a rub with a soft cloth from time to time.

PARQUETRY

Parquetry is a prey to all the ills which beset marquetry — treatment and repairs are carried out in exactly the same manner.

PEWTER

Repairs to pewter can be effected by the soft solder method; an adequate flux can be made by mixing ½oz of glycerine with four or five drops of hydrochloric acid. The cleaned edges of the pieces to be joined are rubbed with emery, fixed in position by means of props, clamps or anything else to hand and coated with the flux.

Lay the soldering metal along the edges to be joined and heat carefully with a large soldering iron or gently burning blow lamp. **Heat must be removed as soon as the solder runs or the pewter is liable to melt.**

Old, well preserved pewter will be found to have a pleasant patination which is best left uncleaned. Just rub this over with a soft cloth to bring up the shine. If the metal is corroded, however, a light rub over with a fine abrasive might be necessary. **Only use the finest of abrasives, such as crocus powder or ordinary whiting for this, as coarser cleansers will leave the surface covered in fine scratches.**

Dents can often be pushed out by hand or with the aid of a small C cramp. They can also be beaten out quite easily, using a ball peen hammer, from the inside or back of the article but be careful — too much hammering will distort the metal and can cause the dent to spread.

Tankards with broken glass bottoms are no great problem. Have a disc of glass cut to the right size and seat this into place with Araldite to make it waterproof. Sometimes it is possible to pry up the edges of the flange which held the old piece of glass and press the metal down again to conceal your repair. This may fail for one of a number of reasons, in which case it would probably be as well to carefully file away one of the flanges completely so that broken, untidy edges are not left.

PICTURES (OIL)

Like that of every other organic thing, the life of a painting is one of steady deterioration. Very often, the degenerative process is so slow as to be virtually unnoticeable even over hundreds of years, but, slow or fast, the process continues. Varnishes bloom and darken, paint cracks and flakes, pigments fade and discolour, even the canvas, paper, wood and various other supports upon which pictures are painted gradually decay and crumble.

Although the process is inevitable, it can be considerably delayed by proper care and attention and, even when fairly well advanced, deterioration can be virtually halted and the damage made good. The extent to which this is carried out, of course, depends greatly upon the present or expected value of the particular work of art under consideration.

Restoration of oil paintings is not something to be rushed into lightly, particularly if the picture is of unknown value.

Assuming, however, that a picture whose value has been established as being small is in need of some work, little is lost by having a go.

An oil painting is built up in layers on a base of canvas, wood or any other material which was available to the artist. The base is usually coated with size, sometimes also with gesso, and then with a number of layers of paint whose final surface is protected by varnish.

Many old paintings need nothing more than cleaning. The varnish coat collects dirt and itself becomes discoloured with age; this may have to be removed and replaced if the discolouration is too bad. The worst possible cleanser for paintings is soap and water — a combination which should never be used.

Possibly one of the best and most reliable of proprietary picture cleansers is marketed by Messrs. Winsor and Newton under the name 'Winton Picture Cleaner'. Needless to say, their very precise instructions should be followed to the letter if the cleaner is to be used safely and effectively.

A good general solvent for picture varnish is composed of five parts of alcohol to three of turpentine and one of ethyl acetate. This is used to moisten a pad of cotton wool which is then lightly wiped across small areas of the painting in a circular motion. The surface

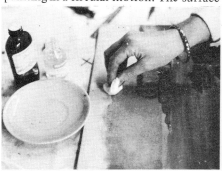

of the cotton wool should be looked at frequently and a clean piece used every time the old becomes coated with varnish. As soon as the slightest trace of

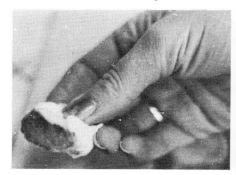

colour appears on the cotton wool, stop and swab the area gently with turpentine to arrest the action of the solvent. In this way, work across the entire surface of the painting but try, if possible, to move from each area before colour is seen on the cotton wool — the aim is to remove almost but not all the old varnish.

White paint tends to discolour rather badly. Once the varnish has been removed, any areas of white can be brightened by applying hydrogen peroxide with a fine brush but care should be taken not to touch any other colours or they will be badly affected.

Wash the entire surface of the picture with turpentine (not turpentine substitute) and allow this to harden before applying a new coat of dammar or mastic varnish.

An alternative method of cleaning is to wipe the entire surface with copaiva balsam and oil of turpentine in one go. This should be repeated several times, allowing several hours to elapse between treatments, finishing to be carried out as above.

Always work in a brightly lit area, preferably by daylight, since subtle differences in colours will often pass undetected in dim light and irreparable damage could be done by removing, for example, an entire layer of brown paint under the mistaken impression that it was merely the discoloured varnish.

It cannot be too strongly emphasised that the outline cleaning method described above should only be used on works of minimal worth. At no time should an amateur attempt the cleaning of any painting of value.

If a canvas is torn, a patch can be applied to the back using an adhesive made of five parts of beeswax, five parts of resin and one part of Venice Turpentine melted together in a double saucepan. **This is an extremely inflammable mixture and should not be melted in an ordinary pan.**

Soak the canvas patch in this mixture and press it onto the back of the canvas with a warm iron. If the iron is too hot, it will blister the paint. Apply pressure to the patch while the adhesive sets and repaint the damaged area as necessary. Before the repainting is done, it might be necessary to fill irregularities in the surface of the painting. Flake white pigment is quite adequate for this, but allow it to dry thoroughly before applying any other paint.

When an old canvas is in poor condition, relining is called for. This simply means removing the old canvas from its stretcher and gluing it onto a piece of new canvas.

First, using a water soluble paste, cover the surface of the painting with two or three layers of clean paper. These can be washed off carefully when the relining is done and they will ensure that the painting remains well protected throughout the process.

Prepare a frame and stretch a new linen canvas over it (the simplest thing to do, of course, is to buy a ready stretched canvas slightly larger than the picture to be relined). Coat this liberally with size and, having cut the old canvas from its stretcher, coat both canvas surfaces with glue and press them together, taking care to smooth out all air bubbles.

Just before the glue is dry iron the two canvasses carefully with a warm iron in order to force the glue well into all crevices.

Finally, remove the canvas from its stretcher and fix it to one of the right size before carefully washing away the paste holding the protective paper on the front of the picture.

The overriding general rule concerning care of paintings is *moderation*. Like good salami, a painting is best hung in a cool, dry atmosphere with good air circulation and in a position shielded from excesses of light. Continual exposure to hot, dry air may cause the paint and the varnish to crack and even flake off the support on which the picture is painted. Exposure to damp encourages the growth of mildew, particularly on canvas and size. It can also affect the varnish, causing an opaque bloom to occur. Excessive light will cause fading and discolouration of certain pigments. A painting subjected to extremes of atmospheric conditions will begin to crack as age destroys the elasticity of the materials used in its creation. A painting clamped too tightly into a close-fitting frame may suffer from warped stretchers, particularly when it is hung or stored in damp conditions. Too prolonged exposure to damp may even cause a loss of adhesion between the paint and its support, causing 'cupping' and flaking. Excessive heat will cause the paint and varnish layers to rise in fragile blisters which are liable to disintegrate at the slightest touch.

Possibly the most dangerous periods in the life of any painting occur just prior to, and after, a sale. Immense care should be taken over the individual packing of each work and adequate insurance cover should be arranged to allow for loss or damage however caused. Before a painting is packed, all hooks and projecting hanging-supports should be carefully removed and the painting should be protected front and back with felt or wadding. Hardboard or plywood panels should be cut slightly larger than the frame and firmly secured to front and back to ensure that the surface of the painting does not suffer from accidental knocks or contact with irregular surfaces during transportation. The only error that can possibly be made is that of inadequate care – it is impossible to err on the side of overprotection.

A common practice which causes damage, particularly to paintings on canvas or other flexible supports, is that of pasting labels onto the reverse side. This can cause uneven expansion and contraction of the support, eventually causing the paint to crack round the outlines of the label. One of the finest protections a painting can be given is a hardboard or plywood backing cut to fit over the back of the stretcher. If this backing has a couple of holes drilled at top and bottom it will fulfill several useful roles. Firstly, of course, it will discourage the habit of labelling or even writing directly onto the reverse surface of the canvas. Secondly, it will help prevent damage to the canvas if the picture is dropped or otherwise mishandled (in this context, it would be impossible to count the number of pictures which have been propped against chairs or other items of furniture prior to being hung, and have then been accidentally knocked so that a projecting corner or handle has been driven through the unprotected canvas). Thirdly, dust is kept from the canvas and, because holes have been drilled top and bottom, air is allowed to circulate freely past the canvas; reducing the risk of mildew and other fungoid growths.

The siting of a painting in a room can be of immense importance, not only from the point of view of interior decor. Positions over radiators or central heating vents should be scrupulously avoided, as should positions subjected to direct or strongly reflected sunlight. The favourite position of all — over the fireplace — is one in which the surface of the painting will receive regular doses of soot and greasy, sometimes corrosive, fumes. Paintings hung in positions where they will be subjected to sudden changes of temperature or humidity are inevitably going to suffer damage, so entrance halls and rooms in which, perhaps, windows are left open at night are best avoided.

By far the best positions, therefore, from the point of view of the paintings themselves, are on sheltered walls in cool rooms, extra light being provided as necessary by means of specially positioned directional light fittings.

PINE FURNITURE (To Strip)

Provided that a little care is exercised, the stripping of pine furniture can be a relatively quick and simple process, but it is as well to have some idea of the nature of the timber before deciding to tackle the job. As a general rule, heavier items will have been made of a good quality pine, straight grained and fairly free from knots and dark, resinous patches and streaks. Flimsier pieces however, will usually reveal poorer quality timber, frequently having large, not very attractive knots, not uncommonly filled with putty and white size. These can be remedied in the finishing stages fairly easily.

Having selected an item for stripping, the job will be greatly simplified by removing all handles, escutcheons and other metal ornamentation. Apart from making the actual item easier to strip, all these small pieces are cleaned far more easily on their own.

Any repairs to the woodwork are best carried out before stripping, since the caustic solution used has a slight staining effect on timber which will help the new wood blend with the old.

Materials

Caustic soda (Obtainable from most ironmongers in 1 lb. tins); **acetic acid** (Vinegar contains a workable solution of acetic acid); **brush** (A nylon bristled long handled washing up brush); **rubber gloves** (Obtainable from any ironmongers); **rubber boots** (Useful as a time saver, allowing a little more freedom in the application of the caustic solution); **cold water** (Preferably a hose running continuously); **old bucket** (Enamel or polythene only).

Technique

Owing to the corrosive nature of caustic soda, it is best to carry out the stripping operation on a well drained concrete floor, keeping a hose flowing throughout.

Since the solution is more effective when it is applied hot, fairly small quantities should be mixed at a time, adding the caustic to the water in the ratio of ·25 of a lb. per quart.

It is extremely dangerous to put water into the caustic soda. Always

add the soda slowly to the water, stirring continuously.

Prime the entire article first with cold water, inside and out, so that the interior will absorb as little of the caustic soda as possible and paint on the caustic solution with the nylon brush, scrubbing well in. It is important to keep the solution away from eyes and any accidental splashes should be immediately washed thoroughly with cold water. Varnish should come off immediately with the first application, but paint may require repeated applications. A pointed knife or screwdriver will be found useful in cleaning cracks and corners.

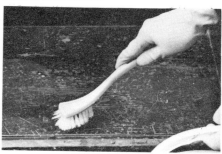

When the paint has been entirely removed, the article should be scrubbed thoroughly with cold water, inside and out, and a final wash down with vinegar or a weak solution of acetic acid (about 2 per cent) will neutralise any remaining caustic.

Any odd red stains and blotches will be found to yield to a firm rub with a household cleanser such as Vim or Ajax.

Dry the article away from direct heat to avoid any risk of warping and cracking and, when it is thoroughly dry, sandpaper thoroughly, finishing with 00 grade flour paper. Any light spots in the timber can be carefully toned down with a little light oak stain applied with a fine watercolour brush. If the wood, after stripping, is too dark for taste it may be lightened with ordinary household bleach, washed thoroughly with water and finished in the usual way with sandpaper and wax or a polyurethane varnish. (Beeswax is generally considered to be best for most pine, as it tends to reduce blemishes slightly).

This plaster figure has been treated with a walnut stain. The open join in the arm could easily be filled with fresh plaster and coloured to match.

PLASTER FIGURES

Plaster figures, being of a fragile nature, are easily broken. Larger figures are usually hollow and repairs to these will follow closely the method used for china repairs except that plaster, being porous and to some extent water soluble, should never be washed with water when it is being cleaned prior to repair.

Owing to the fact that plaster figures are usually finished with a wax polish worked well into the warmed plaster, an alcohol based solvent is the best cleaning medium.

Repairs to plaster figures can be strengthened by patching from the inside with fresh plaster and gauze. To ensure good adhesion between the new plaster and the old, the area to be patched should be thoroughly damped and, if possible, keyed by scratching with a knife point or sharp nail.

Plaster of paris is mixed to the consistency of cream — it should be thin enough to flow when poured but thick enough to cover a hand dipped into it and withdrawn. Strips of gauze or rag are dipped into the plaster and then laid over the repaired area from the inside. Some dispatch is necessary, since the plaster begins to set after a very few minutes.

Missing features can be moulded from available sources or built up directly in plaster. In the latter case, plaster is applied in excess of the amount actually needed and left for a couple of days to dry out thoroughly before being worked with knife and files.

A little dry colour rubbed into the plaster is usually all that is needed to disguise repairs to the state where they are unnoticeable.

A good finish can be restored to plaster by warming the object gently and rubbing a soft or liquid wax polish well in so that it penetrates the porous surface.

PLATE (Sheffield)

Sheffield plate was a method used to reduce the cost of silver objects from 1742 to near the end of the nineteenth century, when electroplating superseded it. It was produced by fusing a thin sheet of silver onto a copper base, the two then being rolled into sheets of the required overall thickness before being made into useful articles.

Naturally, with time, the layer of silver becomes worn, allowing the copper base to show through. When this occurs to an unsightly degree, it is sometimes felt worthwhile to have the piece electroplated, but the advice of a valuation expert should always be sought before this course is embarked upon.

The cleaning of Sheffield plate (as, indeed, any other plated objects) should always be undertaken with care. Remember that even the gentlest of polishes has a slight abrasive action and removes a minute layer of metal — sooner or later wearing completely through the plating to the base metal.

POLISH

Despite the host of instant polishes marketed for the treatment of all kinds of materials, very few — if any — are better than the old, home-made recipes which have been used for generations to build up the rich patina found on a well cared-for antique.

As regards metal polishes, most of the proprietary brands seem to be perfectly satisfactory, though particular care should be taken when selecting a suitable preparation for the treatment of silver.

In the case of furniture polishes, however, far greater care is necessary in their selection. It is generally agreed that the safest and most satisfactory polish to use on antique furniture is a wax based polish. Of the proprietary brands, Antiquax and Goddard's Furniture Cream are widely recommended. An alternative is to make up your own polish by melting — in a double saucepan — 16 parts of beeswax to four of resin and one of Venice turpentine. Care should be taken here because the mixture is inflammable.

Allow to cool and then, while it is still soft, add twelve parts of turpentine. Store in tins with close-fitting lids.

French polish is a preparation of shellac dissolved in spirit. Many authorities deprecate its use and, since it was not introduced until the nineteenth century, it is best not applied to furniture of an earlier date.

Although it is quite simple to mix your own french polish, there is little point, since perfectly satisfactory preparations are widely obtainable. As good as any is that marketed under the Furniglass name.

Before application of french polish, the wood surface must be perfectly clean, dry and smooth. All previous finishes must be removed and irregularities in the surface filled. The wood may be stained provided it is carefully sanded before the polish is applied.

French polish is not brushed or sprayed on, it is applied with a 'rubber'. This consists of a ball of wadding wrapped in a lint-free cotton cloth, folded in such a way that it forms a pear shape, with no edges or corners of the cloth on the polishing surface.

Enough polish is poured from

the bottle onto the rubber so that, when it is squeezed, a small quantity will ooze to the surface.

Starting at one corner, rub the polish into the wood with a figure-of-eight motion, feeding the rubber with more polish as necessary. The object should be to produce a thin, even film over the entire surface.

Once this has hardened it is rubbed down gently with fine garnet paper wrapped round a large-ish sanding block and the process is repeated, this time rubbing with the grain instead of with the figure-of-eight motion.

If, on application of the second and subsequent coats, the rubber is felt to stick, a little linseed oil may be used for lubrication.

There is no standard number of applications to produce a well-finished result — much will depend on the absorbancy of the wood and on the particular polish being used. Generally, however, three to five coats will be required to produce a shine of the right depth.

To increase the shine a final light rub over can be given using pure spirit on a clean rubber. This should be applied lightly and swiftly, as it must not be allowed to soak into the polish. Its purpose is only to smooth the final slight irregularities in the surface.

POLISH (removal of)

The best method of removing any polish is to find the appropriate solvent. In terms of furniture finishes, this is usually quite a simple matter since meths or acetone will remove most finishes.

If a flat area — for example a table top — is to be stripped quickly, there is no better tool than a scraper of the kind used by cabinet makers. This is a piece of 1/16" sheet steel about three inches by five, shaped and sharpened as illustrated. It is most important that the corners of the scraping edge are dulled sufficiently to prevent them scoring the wood.

Held almost upright, the scraper is drawn across the surface, always in the direction of the grain, and experience will soon dictate the amount of pressure to be applied to remove only the wax polish surface or the entire finish from the wood.

RIVETS

Soft metal rivets are commonly used for such purposes as fixing handles to saucepans. Where they have worked loose or fallen out, replacement is a perfectly simple matter. Your new rivet should be at least 1/16th of an inch longer than the thickness of metal and should fit exactly into the hole.

With the rivet in position, rest the head on something solid — the corner of a vice, a small anvil or even a large, flat spanner.

Using a ball peen hammer, tap the projecting end of the rivet gently, working round the edge to produce a slightly domed effect.

PRINTS

See '**Books**' heading.

ROCKERS (To Make and Fit)

A simple, popular and often profitable conversion is frequently carried out on windsor and other kitchen chairs to make them into rocking chairs, using the backs of old broken chairs as the rockers.

The only tricky part of this procedure lies in marking up the rockers correctly so that, when the holes are cut, the legs will fit comfortably into them without being forced out of line.

Remove the finish from the lower ¾" of each of the chair's legs. .

Lay the chair on its side with one rocker placed in position beneath the lower legs. The ends of the legs should overlap the rocker by about ¾".

Mark carefully along each side of each leg and, using a setsquare, carry the marks across the top of the rocker.

Turn the chair over and repeat with the other rocker.

If the legs are round, select a drill bit of suitable diameter; if they are round and tapering, the drill bit should be the same diameter as the thinnest part of the legs.

Mark the rockers for the centre point of the drill bit.

Being careful to drill at the angle indicated by the marks on the sides of the rockers, drive holes to a depth of ¾".

Rectangular legs will be housed in mortices cut in the usual way but, again at the angle dictated by the slope of curve.

Glue the chair legs into the holes cut in the rockers, applying pressure while the glue sets.

Clean off any excess glue, staining and polishing as required to match the colour and finish of the rockers to that of the chair.

RUNGS (Loose and Broken)

If the only thing wrong with a chair is that one of the rungs is loose, a proper repair is hardly worth the time and effort involved; the usual procedure in this case would be to pack the ends of the rung with slivers of glued veneer

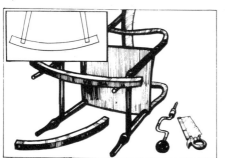

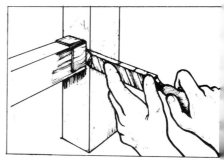

to stop it rattling about, delaying a full scale repair until such time as the chair may need treatment for falling apart. An alternative to simply packing the loose joints with veneer might be to wet or steam the joints in the hope of softening the old glue sufficiently to cause it to re-amalgamate, any play again being taken up with pieces of veneer.

If the rung is of a purely decorative nature and it has broken, it can usually be repaired quite satisfactorily by gluing it in the same manner as a broken arm (See **Arms Broken**), but because some people make a habit of hooking their feet onto chair rungs, this is rarely satisfactory and the odds are that it will break again. Instead, therefore, a new rung should be fitted, even though this entails the removal of legs.

Depending on the style and value of the chair, the new rung may simply be a piece of dowel rod stained to match or it may be a piece of the appropriate wood shaped or even carved to resemble as closely as possible the broken member.

Remove the front legs from the chair, using a padded hammer as described under the "**Falling Apart**" heading, and clean all old glue from the housings into which the rung fits and from the joints which will have to be reglued when the legs are rejoined.

Having made the new rung and fitted it dry to ensure that it was properly cut and a good fit, glue all joints and re-assemble the chair in one session, applying pressure to ensure good adhesion.

It may be found to be easier if the new rung is stained and finished to match the rest of the chair before it is fitted; certainly, if the colour is a little tricky, it is easier to handle the rung on its own, particularly in the case of one which is carved.

Generally speaking, it will be necessary to fake the age of the new rung to some extent if it is not to appear too obviously the result of a repair job. This can be done in various ways but the essential point is to simulate the wear to which most chair rungs have been subjected during their lifetimes.

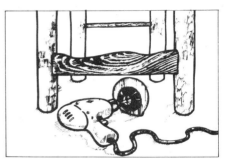

A power drill with a good, coarse sanding disc will cut away the wood unevenly from the upper surfaces of the rung and carefully applied colour will darken the ends. Faking age is an art unto itself and, like most arts, it depends more on observation than on manual dexterity. Look at the old, broken rung or at the rungs on other, similar chairs. You will see that they never wear evenly and symmetrically. You will observe, too, that colour never fades smoothly from light to dark.

RUSHWORK

Rushwork responds to all the same treatments as cane — a good scrub with soap and water will remove most dirt and the addition of a little household bleach to the water will take care of most stains and help with the colour, particularly if the cleaning job is done outside on a summer's day and the rush-work left to dry in the sun.

Loose pieces can be glued down with Evo Stik or the rushwork can be treated with an acrylic varnish — either gloss or matt — which will do much to tidy up frayed areas.

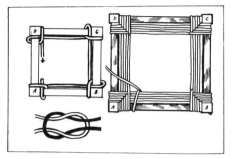

Rushwork seats are not at all difficult to replace, provided the ma-terial — it is called sea grass — can be found. Good craft shops are probably the best bet here, or perhaps up-holsterers' suppliers.

Sea grass is bought by the skein. The easiest way of handling it when actually working on a seat is to wind it onto a piece of wood — about twelve inches long by four wide — the ends of which have had 'V' shaped cuts made in them.

The work is begun by tying the loose end of the sea grass onto the front rail of the seat at the left-hand end as you face it. The knot should be underneath the rail and close to its inside edge. Bring the sea grass up, over the side-rail from the inside, round and across the seat to pass over the right-hand seat rail.

This pattern is repeated until the entire seat is covered.

SCREWS (Removal Of)

Screws that have been in wood for a long time have very often corroded slightly, causing them to be difficult to remove.

Before applying excessive force, always clean out the groove thoroughly to allow the screwdriver a maximum area against which to push. Choose the largest screwdriver whose bit will fit the slot — beside giving you more purchase, this will reduce the risk of damage to the head of the screw. Try turning the screw both ways; because the screwdriver is tending to push the screw into the wood, it is sometimes easier to drive the screw a quarter turn or so further into the wood than it is to withdraw it straight away. The slight-est turn in either direction will break the bond between the screw and the wood, allowing it to be withdrawn fairly easily.

If the screw cannot be budged, fit the screwdriver into its slot and hit the handle sharply with a hammer. This, too, tends to break the bond between screw and wood.

Another method involves heating a poker to red heat and applying it carefully to the head of the screw in an effort to cause it to expand; the theory being that, as the screw cools, it will shrink away from the wood making withdrawal easy.

SHADING

There are two main uses for the techniques of shading; one is to add depth and interest to marquetry designs by darkening pieces of veneer to repre-sent shadow areas, the other is to unevenly darken a repair or an entire piece of furniture in order to give it the appearance of having a greater age than it actually possesses.

Although, in the past, various techniques have been employed for this purpose, including burial of objects in hot sand, the more usual methods are those involving applications of colour which, at its worst, produces the hideous effect to be seen on cheap reproduction furniture.

Dry colours of various shades can be used and a reasonable mixture can be made by mixing three tablespoonfuls of ground dry colour with two of turpentine and three of varnish.

Raw umber is probably about the most widely used base colour, to which burnt sienna may be added in varying proportions to give increasingly warmer tones. Other colours may be added or substituted to blend with the particular wood under treatment, but it should be remembered that it is really the grime of ages that is being simulated and grime is very much the same, no matter what the colour of the wood beneath.

Bearing in mind the effect of years of use and polishing, the centres of panels, exposed edges and high areas of carving are usually found to be of a lighter colour than less accessible areas. This effect is simulated by applying a coat of the coloured varnish and then, before it dries, rubbing it off with a cloth from the highlight areas.

On genuinely old pieces of furniture,. this highlighting effect is never symmetrical and it is this fact which lets down most beginners in their early attempts at faking age. Observation and experiment are the two great teachers which no amount of written instruction can supplant.

Another method of shading to simulate age (and one which should never be undertaken lightly) is to actually char the wood slightly with a blow lamp. Once again, the only way to perfect the technique is to practice it. This method has some advantages over that mentioned above, since it is almost impossible to darken wood evenly with a blowlamp — sharp corners will tend to burn rather quicker than flat surfaces and the softer parts of the grain will darken rather more than the hard parts. Charring will have the effect of contouring wood, causing knots to stand slightly proud of the surrounding surface — another typical age characteristic.

A good strong solution of caustic soda will add years to many woods — some more than others — but it tends to play havoc with the surface.

SHELLAC

Shellac is a kind of resin obtained from an insect, Cocus Lacca. It is normally obtainable in thin plates, orange in colour, which may be dissolved in alcohol. In this form it is widely used as a varnish.

Shellac varnish tends to discolour, particularly if kept in metal containers or exposed to moisture. For this reason it is best stored in glass or stoneware bottles tightly stoppered.

Of great use in repairing dents and other blemishes in wood, shellac sticks are made in a wide variety of shades. The technique for using them requires considerable practice but, once mastered, is invaluable.

Heat is used to melt a small quantity of shellac (a small spirit lamp is ideal) which is caught on a heated knife blade and transferred to the area being repaired. This process is repeated until the shellac has built up sufficiently to stand proud of the surrounding surface. When it has cooled, excess shellac is removed with a sanding block and a finish applied to match that of the piece under repair.

SILVER

To test an object for silver, file a spot in a concealed area deep enough that, if the object is plated, you will be certain to reach the base metal. Apply a drop of nitric acid; standard quality silver will produce a greyish deposit, lower grades giving progressively darker deposits and base metal a green deposit. Wash the area immediately and dry it.

Silver may be cleaned with jeweller's rouge or any good quality proprietary brand of silver cleaner, all of which will remove tarnish in normal circumstances. Another method of removing tarnish is that frequently employed in catering establishments where egg stained forks present a daily problem; a large jar or bowl is lined with aluminium foil (a handful or two of milk bottle tops works equally well) and filled with hot water. Washing soda crystals are then added — a heaped tablespoonful to a two pound jam jar is ample — and the objects to be cleaned immersed in this. It is important that each piece of silver should be actually touching the aluminium foil or bottle tops, since the cleaning is the result of an electro-chemical process. When the tarnish has disappeared, wash the objects in running water and dry them.

Once silver is clean, it can be lacquered with Frigilene or other proprietary brand of silver lacquer and this will keep it looking bright for a year or so depending on the atmosphere in which it is kept — naturally, this applies only to decorative silver, not flat ware.

SLATS

Slats in the backs of chairs are normally made to float — that is, they are not glued into position but simply inserted into slots — since, if they were not, the everyday process of expansion and contraction would tend to cause damage to the structure of the chair.

A missing slat has usually been broken itself or the side of the slot into which it fitted has been broken out.

New slats can be made from any suitable wood and, since a chair usually has more than one, the others can be used to make a pattern. With care, the new slat can be made to spring into its housing, allowing its insertion without the inconvenience of taking the chair to pieces.

Measure carefully the distance between the two fixed members into which the slat slots and also measure the depths of the two slots into which it fits. The length of your new slat should be the distance between the two fixed members plus three quarters of the combined depth of the slots. By pushing one end of the slat fully home and bending it carefully, the other end will be found to fit fairly comfortably into its housing where it will remain — unless subjected to considerably more pressure than it will receive in normal use.

When the housing has broken away, cut the wood back to remove any splinters, leaving a clean, square edged area to be filled.

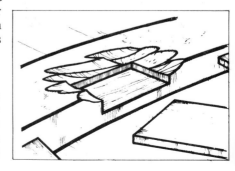

Cut a piece of wood of the correct type to a size that will exactly fill the prepared area. Leave the new piece of wood slightly thicker than it needs to be, this can be pared down later.

Replace the slat, or, if it is missing, make a new one and lay it in position.

Glue your prepared piece of wood into place and apply pressure while the glue sets. It will not matter that the slat becomes glued to the fixed member provided that one end remains free in its housing.

When the glue has dried, pare away excess wood from the piece you have just inserted, sanding it down and staining and polishing to match the old wood.

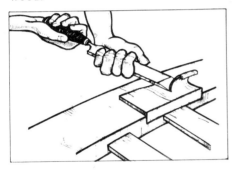

SOLDER

Soldering is the method used to join two pieces of metal by means of another molten metal which, as it cools and hardens, will adhere to the surfaces being joined.

For ease of description, solders are broadly divided into two kinds; hard and soft. Hard solder, as the name implies, is harder than soft solder and it has a higher melting point, necessitating the use of a blow lamp or other

direct heating method for its use. Soft solder, with its relatively low melting point, is used to join metals whose melting point is also low, heat being usually applied by means of a soldering iron.

To assist adhesion between solder and the metals to be joined, a flux is used. This is a substance which prevents the heated metals from forming oxides. Much softer solder can be bought with a core of flux running through it for ease of application.

When soft soldering, it is important that the iron used should be large enough for the job in hand; too small an iron will give up its heat too quickly to the surrounding metal, preventing the solder from running.

The method of working is to heat the soldering iron sufficiently so that, when solder is brought into contact with the copper bit, it will melt and flow. The spreading of solder on the bit is called tinning. When the bit has been tinned, it is held in contact with the metal to be joined and solder is applied to the copper bit, when it will melt and run onto the joint.

It is, of course, essential that the joint be clean and free from grease. The best method of ensuring that this is so is to abrade it with a fine file, and the copper bit of the soldering iron should be so treated each time it is used.

Hard solder, as has been mentioned already, needs a blow lamp or other source of direct heat. Borax and water are used to make a flux, and spelter — a zinc/copper alloy usually obtained in granules — is used as the solder. The join is thoroughly cleaned and the flux and solder are laid along it before being brought up to the required red heat with a blowlamp, or, for larger pieces, a forge.

STAIN

Wood stains are these days widely available in all colours from antique oak to Chelsea orange; they may be composed of natural or synthetic colouring matter and they may be water or spirit miscible. Every Do it Yourself shop seems to stock a few colours of either kind but almost no shops stock them all — one of the unfortunate results of manufacturers offering too wide a selection.

Although most manufacturers produce stains labelled 'Mahogany', 'Light Oak', 'Walnut' and so on, some degree of colour mixing is almost always necessary to produce exactly the colour required for a piece of furniture. This is something that only experience can teach fully, but a few minutes spent experimenting with combinations of stains on different woods will always prove worthwhile. A typical example of this is mahogany. Most proprietary stains labelled 'Mahogany' are red pure and simple — perfect if you want a technicolour table top glowing like a ripe cherry in the middle of the room but not so good if you want a table top that looks like mahogany. The addition of some dark oak or walnut stain will be found to make all the difference.

Before any wood can be stained, it must first be stripped thoroughly of all old polish and finishes (see appropriate heading) and sanded to a perfect smoothness.

If spirit based stains are to be used, they can be applied immediately. Water based stains, however, will raise the grain of the wood and if they are to be used, it is first necessary to wet the surface to be stained with clean water and allow it to dry. When it is dry, it will have a rough feel and should be sanded down with flour paper.

Repeat this at least once, preferably twice.

Apply the stain with a brush working it well into the grain. If in doubt as to darkness, always err on the light side and give another coat later if necessary.

To prevent the end grain from absorbing too much stain and appearing unnaturally dark when the job is finished, give it a quick coat of shellac, before staining. The shellac will soak into the wood without sealing it completely and the stain will not absorb as thoroughly as it would on untreated wood. This only works on the end grain — if the shellac gets anywhere else, it will prevent the stain from reaching the wood.

Usually, as soon as the stain is dry, it can be polished. For water-based stains this will take about twenty four hours, spirit-based stains are dry as soon as they look dry — a matter of minutes usually. Sometimes, a water-based stain will cause a slight raising of the grain — even though steps have been taken to prevent this. There is no alternative, in this case, to resanding lightly with flour paper before polishing.

TAMBOUR

Although tambours may look rather daunting things to repair or renew, they are, in fact, surprisingly simple.

Remove the old tambour by taking off the handles or projecting lip from the leading edge and feeding it through to the rear of the desk.

You will need a piece of canvas cut to the same size as that being replaced. If the original tambour is missing, the size of the piece of canvas can be measured quite easily. Measure the width between the inside surfaces of the sides of the desk. The length is measured along the grooves in which the tambour slides from front to back of the desk. Measure from the desk top to the point where the tambour disappears from view and add about three inches.

If all the wooden slats are there, these need merely cleaning up and gluing to the canvas backing, though great care must be taken to ensure that they are placed absolutely straight and square to the run. A good idea is to make up a half frame — perhaps by tacking two pieces of wood onto adjacent sides of a work bench — against which all the slats can be precisely placed.

Position the canvas carefully on the workbench top (which must, of course, be flat and smooth) and spread over it a thin layer of contact adhesive. Apply contact adhesive, too, to all the slats, leaving their ends clean so that their free-running will not be impaired when replaced in their grooves

When the adhesive has dried, press the slats carefully, one at a time, into position on the canvas.

All that remains is to stain and polish the slats as necessary, and feed in the tambour from the rear of the piece. Handles or knobs are fitted last.

TORTOISESHELL

Treatment for tortoiseshell is generally much the same as that for **Horn**.

TUNBRIDGE WARE

The two commonest faults developed by Tunbridge ware are a darkening of the varnish coat and the loss of sections of mosaic. The first of these is relatively easy to put right, the second less so.

When the varnish has darkened to an unsightly degree and the decision is made to remove it, first check the piece extremely carefully to ensure that all pieces of veneer are held securely in place. If not, glue them down in the manner described under the **Marquetry** heading. If any pieces are missing you may be able to replace them but the task is likely to be difficult, owing to their small size and the intricacy of many designs.

Where a large section of design is missing, the best repair method might be to cut a single piece of light-coloured (e.g. birch) veneer to fit.

Having replaced all missing pieces, remove the old varnish by scraping carefully with a razor blade, sharp chisel or pieces of broken glass. Naturally this must be carried out with great care, so as not to dislodge any pieces of veneer or score the surface of the wood.

When all varnish is removed, rub over carefully with flour paper until the surface is perfectly smooth and flat.

At this point, assuming that you have replaced a section of the pattern with a piece of birch veneer, you may be able to fake the pattern with pencil, indian ink and water-colour. When this is dry, give a coat of clear varnish and leave the piece in a dust-free atmosphere to dry.

When the varnish is dry, you might find that the grain of the wood has been raised, or that some areas have absorbed the varnish. In this case, sand gently with fine garnet paper until the whole surface is perfectly smooth. Wipe away all dust and re-varnish.

UPHOLSTERY

Upholstery is one of those jobs which many people would like to tackle, only to be discouraged by the apparent complexity of the task. In fact, the re-upholstery of, say, a button-back chair is not particularly difficult.

Perhaps it is best thought of as a series of separate jobs, each to be completed before the next is begun. In this way, confidence in your own abilities will be kept high and the chances of success will dramatically increase.

To describe the method of upholstering a chair from scratch is beyond the scope of this book. More commonly, however, a chair will be found whose seat or covering material needs replacing.

Before actually beginning the task of re-upholstering a chair, it is important to understand how the job will be carried out in sections, a piece at a time. Measuring up helps to do this, since the material will be applied in separate pieces, and each piece represents a particular stage in the progress toward the finished job.

Basic tools and materials needed for upholstery are:
tape measure, mallet, magnetic upholsterer's hammer, shears, pincers, an old screwdriver, a craft knife with a new blade, upholsterer's needles and regulator, skewers, ½ inch tacks, 5/8 inch tacks, sisal string, buttoning twine, webbing. flock, hessian, buttons (cloth-backed are best. Always buy a few more than you will need in case of breakage), upholstery material.

MEASURING
Inside Back

First, push the tape between the seat and back, in the middle of the chair, to a depth of about four inches — you will feel the wooden frame to which the material will later be tacked. Run the tape up the back of the chair, pushing it well into all button cavities in its path, (in most cases, two) over the top and about three inches down the outside of the back. When there are no existing button cavities, allow 1½ inches for each button you intend to insert.

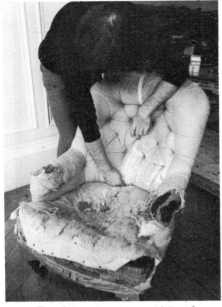

To determine the width of material for the inside back, take a measurement just above the arms, again pressing well into button cavities or adding 1½ inches per button (in this case, four). Allow three inches extra on each side to carry round to the back.

Inside Arms

Press the tape into the rearmost button on one arm. Carry it forward round the front of the arm and allow three inches extra. Now measure from the side edge of the seat straight up the arm at the highest point, allowing four inches extra.

Seat

Press tape to a depth of four inches between the seat and centre of the back. Carry it forward and down the front of the seat to the bottom of the wood frame. Add an extra three inches or so to be taken up when the seat is padded.

The width measurement is taken straight over the front (i.e., the widest point) down to the bottom of the wood frame on each side. Alow four inches extra for padding.

Outside Back

Measure from top to bottom of the outside back at its highest point. Add an extra two inches.

The width is measured right round the outside of the chair from the front of one arm to the front of the other. It is quite possible that this measurement will exceed the width of any available material. In this case, the usual method is to add a small piece at the bottom of each side to make up the required width.

Cutting Out

When cutting the material, it is important to remember that the weft must run across the back and seat, and from front to back of the arms. When a velvet material is used, the nap should brush downward on the back and arms, forward on the seat.

Do not attempt to cut the material to shape, simply leave it in rectangular pieces. Trimming is carried out actually on the chair as each piece of material is fixed.

Having measured and cut the material, lay it on one side while the chair is stripped down prior to re-upholstering.

Begin by turning the chair upside down and removing the entire seat. Using a tack-remover (an old screwdriver will do) knock out all tacks by inserting the blade under each head in turn, striking the tool handle with a mallet so that the tack is pushed out in the same direction as the grain of the wood — **not** across the grain.

It is quite possible that you will not be the first person to re-upholster your chair. In this case, you could find that there are some old tacks left in the frame. If you are unable to remove these, tap them well in out of the way.

You will probably find that the springs are removable. If so, cut them free from the webbing and from each other. If necessary, clean them of rust.

Once the seat has been stripped away, clean and repair the legs and any woodwork which will be visible after the upholstery has been replaced, repolishing where necessary.

The first replacement will be the webbing. Since this is a sprung seat, the webbing is tacked across the bottom of the frame.

The strips are stretched tightly across the frame and interlaced for their mutual support. Although a web-stretching tool is made, its use can cause the webbing to be stretched too tightly. A man should be able, by pulling hard, to create sufficient tension without the use of such a tool.

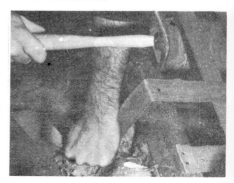

Webs are secured at each end by five tacks (use 5/8 inch improved tacks for this) placed as shown.

When the webbing is all in place, turn the chair over and position the springs as shown in the photograph. Sew each to the webbing at three equally-spaced points.

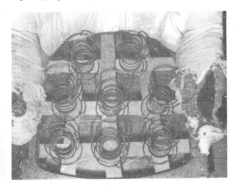

Now, with strong string, tie the centres of the springs and tack the ends of the string to the chair frame. The string should not be slack, but it should not depress the springs appreciably. This prevents the springs from slopping about laterally as the chair is used, ensuring that the seat remains comfortable and shapely.

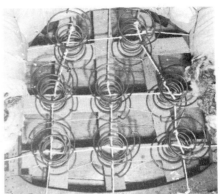

Cut a piece of heavy-duty hessian large enough to cover the seat and be tacked down to the frame all round. Turn the edges under, say about 1 inch and place tacks 1½ inches apart, pulling the hessian just tight enough to cause a slight compression of all the springs.

Using your sacking needle, tie the spring tops to the hessian, each spring to be secured at three points. This prevents the springs from bending laterally, ensuring that they take the weight of sitters evenly.

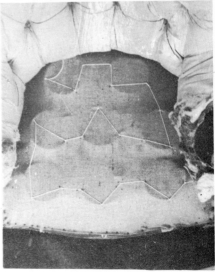

Now thread a piece of string all the way round the seat, leaving loops under which stuffing will be packed.

Tuck horsehair all the way round the gulley to build up the seat's shape. Then lay a two inch mat of horsehair all over the seat.

BURLAP

Cut a second piece of hessian to cover the seat again, allowing about four inches all round. Lay this over the seat and temporarily tack the front with a few tacks driven only halfway in.

Using ½ inch tacks, secure the hessian to the top of the frame starting at the back, pulling it firmly but not too tight and turning the edge under. By now, the seat should be taking its characteristic shape.

NOTE Now using the regulator, adjust the shape of the padding along the front edge. Withdraw the temporary tacks and, turning the surplus hessian under, tack it finally. This row of tacks should be placed in the upper surface of the front rail. The hessian should not be allowed to overlap the front rail, as this would cause unsightly bulges in the finish. BURLAP

Trim all surplus hessian from back and sides. Using the regulator, pull the stuffing toward the edges, evening out lumps and filling any hollows that can be felt.

With the ten inch needle, sew the stuffing in place by passing the thread down through the seat, through the webbing, underneath, along, and back up through the seat to produce a result as shown in the photograph.

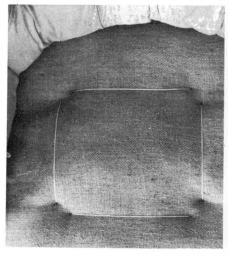

Again using the ten inch needle, run a blanket stitch along the lower front edge of the seat without the thread breaking the upper surface of the hessian. The diagram shows how this is done. The purpose is to pull and hold the stuffing close to the front edge.

Again adjust the stuffing.

Now, a third row of stitches is put in, entering above the first two and emerging in front of the second. This finishes the front of the seat in such a way that it will keep its shape without sagging.

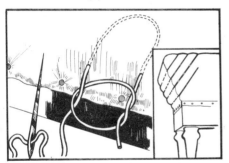

Use the regulator to pull stuffing forward so that the upper front edge of the seat stands about ½ inch forward of the wooden frame.

Half an inch above the first row of stitches put in another, this time breaking the upper surface.

Now turn your attention to the inside·back of the chair. It is most unlikely that the back will need rebuilding. If it does, the procedure is much the same as for the seat, the shape being built up and stitched into place.

If the chair has not previously been buttoned, these can be put in without alteration to the existing stuffing. Simply by cutting holes in the hessian at the appropriate spots and proceding as follows.

Poke your finger into the stuffing to make cavities where the buttons are to go. The usual arrangement is to have four rows of buttons. The top row has three; the second, four. The third row has three and the bottom row, four. The middle button of the top and third rows are placed on a line which bisects the back vertically. The bottom row runs along the line joining the points at which the arms meet the back. The distance from the bottom row of buttons to the seat should be about the same as the distance between the upper row and the top of the chair back.

Now lay a fresh piece of black felt over the inside back and re-poke the cavities. Cut two inch squares of webbing or hessian, one for each hole (in this case, twenty one in all).

Cut a piece of upholstery material for the back according to the measurement taken earlier.

Lay the material evenly over the back (if it is velvet, make sure the pile runs downward). The top of the material should overhang the back of the chair by about two inches.

If the job is to be done satisfactorily, it is essential that the buttons be put on in the order shown. Poking

thread it on to the other end of the twine. Push it through the back of the button and again through the chair. Tie the threads in a slip-knot, roll up a piece of webbing and pull the knot fairly tight over the roll of webbing. This prevents the threads from pulling through the hessian at the rear of the chair.

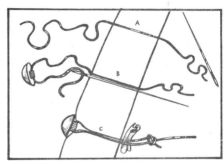

Repeat the process with the rest of the buttons in the order shown.

Always arrange the creases to and from each button as you insert it. Creases always fold downward. Watch the run of the material, ensuring that it runs vertically. Failure to do this will cause an excess of material at one side of the chair-back and a shortage at the other.

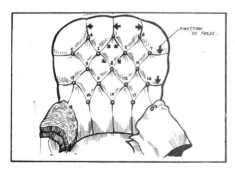

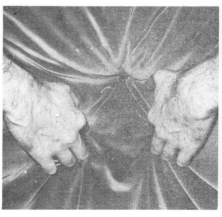

the material well into the first cavity, run a thread right through from front to back. Take the needle off and

Once all the buttons are in place, turn the edges of the material round the back and secure with skewers. At the bottom push loose material down behind the seat, leaving it to hang free for now.

Now cover the arms. Lay your material over one arm with the nap running downward. Fold under the edge nearest the back and push in the rear button cavity.

Continue as for the back.

Repeat with the other arm. You will have to cut the material a little at the bottom to push it past the arm supports.

Now, using a tacking stitch, sew the material onto the outside of the chair, trimming off all surplus.

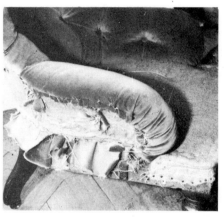

Now lay a pad of horsehair (about one inch thick) over the seat. Cover this with a similar-sized pad of black felt. Tuck both well down into the gully at back and sides. These pads make the final shape of the seat. It is essential, therefore, that they are smooth and free from lumps.

Cut the material for the seat, making cuts in the edges to correspond with the back and arm supports.

Tuck the edges of the material through, between seat, back and arms.

A little time should be spent smoothing the material over the seat and down the front and sides to ensure that there is no slackness and no creases. Remember that the nap must run from back to front.

Tack the back of the seat covering to the frame then, moving to the front, pull the material firmly forward and down inserting three temporary tacks underneath the frame.

Move round the chair, tacking the material to the underside of the frame. Tacks should be spaced evenly, about 1½ inches apart. Keep the material smooth and fairly tight over the seat, but do not stretch it. Remember to check that the warp runs

straight from back to front, the weft from side to side. All final adjustments must be made to the shape of the seat now. Even to the extent of pushing in extra pieces of padding.

Once the material has been tacked to back and sides, remove the temporary tacks from the front and tack it down properly, leaving corners till last.

Tack the corners closely, working toward the front.

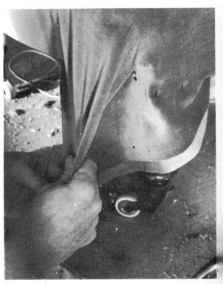

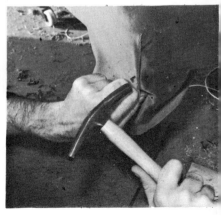

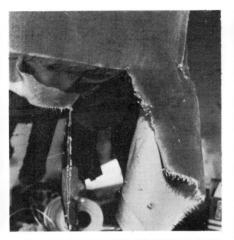

Returning to the inside back, pull all the loose material firmly downward between seat and back, seat and arms. Tack these to the outside edge of the frame and trim off neatly. While the left hand is pulling the material downward, the right should be adjusting the folds below the lowest row of buttons.

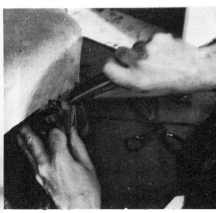

Once this has been done, the tension on the buttons is adjusted by means of the slip-knotted threads hanging down the outside back. As each button is adjusted, tie the threads with any kind of knot that will not slip, and trim the ends.

Now tilt the chair forward and lay a piece of black felt over the outside back.

Cut the material for the outside back, adding pieces to the width as necessary to allow it to extend to the fronts of the arms.

Lay this in position, turning under about ½ inch at the highest point. Secure the top tightly with skewers.

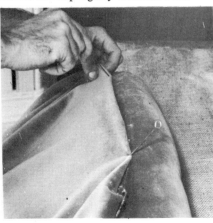

Using the curved needle, slip-stitch the top of the material to the overhang from the inside back, removing skewers as you go.

Work a few inches either side of the centre and then, putting the bottom of the material gently downward, put in some temporary tacks starting from the middle and working outward to below the ends of the arms.

Trim the material roughly to follow the line of the arms and back, allowing two inches over for safety's sake. Turn this under and secure with a few skewers as necessary.

Return to the top of the chair and continue to slipstitch the outside back material to the overhang from the inside. The seam should follow, and should be within one inch of, the curve of the chair. This stitching must be done neatly, since the seam is visible.

Once the seam is completed, the job is almost done.

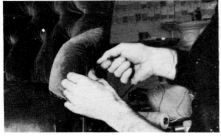

All that remains is to cut a piece of hessian and tack it to the underside of the chair (turning the edges under for neatness) and finish off with a length of braid running right round the lower edge of the frame.

The finished chair.   A day's work has transformed it from a junkyard refugee into an elegant piece of furniture worth more than double the combined cost of the original chair and the materials used.

VENEER

Veneers are thin sheets of wood used either in the manufacture of plywood or as a means of improving the appearance of a piece of furniture.

In furniture making, the veneers used are selected primarily for their decorative effect; either in large sheets, to cover carcasses made of less exotic woods; as inlays; or in small pieces carefully cut and pieced together to make marquetry or parquetry designs.

Repairs to inlays, marquetry and parquetry are described under their own headings. As regards overall veneering, the commonest trouble is that of blistering. This may be due to heat or damp or a combination of the two.

If the blister is unbroken, the simplest and best repair is to cut through the centre of the blister with a scalpel or razor blade — cutting along the grain — and work a quantity of glue under the veneer with a thin spatula (an artist's palette knife is ideal).

Having ensured that the glue reaches to the full extent of the blister, lay a piece of oiled paper — or the greased paper in which cornflakes are kept oven fresh and table ready — over the blister and apply pressure.

If the blister occurs on a curved surface, pressure can be applied best by cutting a block to match the curve and applying pressure to this (see illustration). For concave surfaces, the block may not be necessary, a strong polythene bag filled with sand being a suitable substitute.

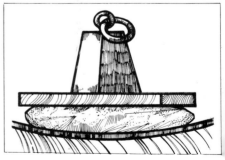

If the blister is old and broken there will probably be a quantity of dust and dirt between the veneer and the base wood. In this case, the veneer will have to be lifted sufficiently for this to be cleaned away. Generally speaking, the answer is to cut the veneer as illustrated, lifting the flaps and proceeding as above once all dirt has been removed.

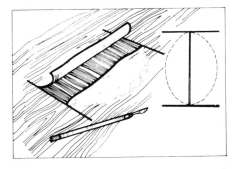

When the edges of a veneered piece are chipped, it is rarely practical to cut small pieces of veneer and apply patches (though this, done properly is a satisfactory procedure). Coloured wax or shellac dripped into the gaps, rubbed down and polished is the quickest and easiest method of repair.

WARPED WOOD

Wood warps for one reason only; its moisture content is unevenly distributed. A simple experiment to demonstrate this is to take a short length of dry, seasoned wood and lay it overnight on a wet cloth. By the morning, the water will have penetrated the fibres on the underside of the wood, causing them to swell and force the wood to curve up at the edges.

If the piece of wood is then turned over, the wetting of the other side will tend to straighten the curve.

This explains why it is that table tops always warp so that the edges curl up and not down; the waterproof finish on the upper surface prevents most damp penetration while the unfinished underside encourages it.

To flatten a warped table leaf, then, remove it from the table and, in the summer, lay it concave side downward on a damp lawn, letting the sun shine on it. The balance of moisture will gradually correct itself and the wood will straighten. If the warp is extreme, or if the wood has also developed a twist, lay some fairly heavy weights on it to assist nature.

If this method is impractical, the leaf can be laid in any warm place and damp rags used to cover the concave side.

Once the wood is flat, allow it to dry freely in an even temperature for a few days and then, before fixing it back onto the table, seal the underside thoroughly with any good proprietary brand of wood sealer.

If, as it dries, the wood regains some of its former curve, repeat the damping process and continue it past the point at which the curve flattens out, again leaving it to dry for a few days. It is most important that the wood be allowed to dry naturally and slowly, in order that its moisture content can balance itself out.

WATCHES

There is almost nothing that the unskilled amateur can do to improve the performance of an antique watch — even suitably-qualified professionals are difficult to find.

General cleaning and minor repairs to case or face, however, can often be tackled with safety, provided that the movement is first removed. Never attempt to remove the movement of any watch unless you know how — different movements are removed in different ways and you should always seek the advice of someone who knows the correct method for your particular watch.

Cases can be cleaned according to the materials of which they are made (see, for example, **Gold, Silver, Enamel** headings) and minor repairs may, perhaps, be effected.

One of the commonest faults developed by watch cases involves the clogging of hinges and springs with dirt, which prevents their easy opening or closure. Clean these with lighter fuel carefully applied and oil them sparingly with a little light oil. Keep such oiling to a minimum, since excess oil can seep into the watch mechanism and clog it.

New glasses should be left to the professional, since they need to be carefully ground into the bezel.

Chipped enamel dials may be treated in the same way as clock dials (see **Clocks** heading).

WAX FIGURES

Hand carved wax model of a foxhound, signed A.G. Haigh, overall height, 14ins.

By virtue of the material of which they are made, wax figures are extremely delicate. Prevention always being better than cure, the best treatment for wax figures, fruit or any similar objects is to keep them under

glass and away from all heat and direct light.

When cleaning is felt to be essential, try first a gentle brushing with a soft brush (e.g. a water-colourist's wash brush). This will remove all loose dirt and may prove sufficient alone. If not, check carefully the way the model has been coloured. If, as is often the case, the wax itself is coloured, cleaning may be continued. Where superficial colour has been applied, no further cleaning must be attempted.

Having made certain that the colour is not superficial, try brushing the wax gently with a soft paintbrush dipped in cool water to which a little detergent has been added.

Repairs should always be left to an expert. Any attempts at melting broken pieces together or dripping paraffin wax onto damaged areas are doomed to failure — and possibly worse.

WAX STICKS

To make wax sticks, melt three parts of beeswax and one of paraffin wax (these proportions are by weight, not volume). After removal from the heat, dry colours are added to approximate the colour of any wood to be filled. This is largely a matter of trial and error, since the colour of a piece of furniture is determined not only by the wood and stain used in its manufacture, but also by the treatment it has received during its lifetime. As a general rule, it is better to err on the light side since this can always be corrected during finishing.

Mix the colours and wax very thoroughly and then, just before it sets, pour the mixture into a shallow tray or dish. Cut it into handy sized strips before it goes hard and store these in a jar away from dust and direct sunlight.

WEAPONS

As many a military man has learned to his cost, one of the greatest ills to which weapons are subject is rust. Since it is easier to guard against rust than cure it, the obvious (yet not always followed practice) is to keep all iron and steel weapons protected from damp with a thin film of Vaseline, light oil or lacquer.

Before attempting to clean or restore any weapon, advice should be sought as to its value and the advisability of the treatment you intend to carry out: many collectors prefer that weapons remain uncleaned and you may well be reducing the cash value of a piece by improving its decorative value.

When pieces of little value are found to be in a rusty condition, they should be stripped down as far as possible and have their rusty parts immersed in paraffin (of course parts made of wood, leather or other organic material should not be subjected to this treatment). Soaking may be continued as long as necessary, but 24 hours should be sufficient, particularly if badly rusted areas are rubbed vigourously with a wire brush at two-hourly intervals. Where immersion is not possible, apply paraffin with a brush or rag to rusted spots for a couple of days.

On removing the piece from the paraffin, treat all rusted areas with a wire brush, taking care that no damage is done to any silver or gilt work, or to brass bindings. This is a messy business and so best carried out in old clothes outside the house.

After wire brushing has removed most of the rust, use steel wool or

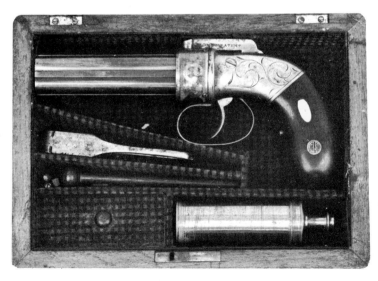

Guns of all kinds are very much collectors' items and should be kept as nearly as possible in their original condition. (Wallis & Wallis)

Showing how a Japanese sword handle is removed. No Japanese sword should be cleaned or restored before the advice of a valuation expert has been sought. (Wallis & Wallis).

emery paper, lubricated with light oil, to tackle particularly stubborn areas.

If the metal has been blued, this treatment will remove it. Blueing

solutions are obtainable from gunsmiths who will advise on their use.

Once all rust has been removed, wash the pieces in very hot water and detergent, drying them thoroughly before polishing with metal polish and coating them with your chosen protective preparation.

Wooden, leather and other parts will receive treatment according to their materials.

WOODWORM

There is no need to list the damage that woodworm can do during the two years of their lives spent as grubs inside a piece of furniture. Fortunately, there are plenty of reliable insecticides made specifically for the treatment of furniture both before and during infestation.

The best known of these is undoubtedly Rentokil Woodworm Fluid, which can be obtained in cans fitted with injector nozzles.

Remove all drawers from the piece to be treated and remove all dirt and dust from all surfaces. To ensure that the fluid will not adversely affect colour or finish, test on an out-of-the-way part of the piece of furniture before proceeding with treatment.

Assuming that all is well, liberally coat every surface with the fluid. Pay particular attention to underside, cracks and corners.

If this is not practical, buy an injector and use this to squirt fluid into all worm holes.

After 24 hours, wipe all fluid off with a clean cloth. Keep the piece of furniture under observation for a couple of weeks and at first sign of continued woodworm activity, repeat the treatment.

A

Abrasives 11
Acids 11
Accumulator acid 26
Acetic acid 11, 12, 33
Acetone 38, 58
Acrylic Paint 55
Acrylic Varnish 58
Adhesives (uses of) 69
Adhesive tape 38, 39
Alabaster 12
Alcohol 29, 86
Alcohol stains 24
Almond oil 27, 67
Aluminium foil 98
Amber 13
Ammonia 12, 29, 50
Ammonium Chloride 33
Amyl acetate 58
Antiqueing 99
Antiquing 95, 97
Araldite 19, 33, 50, 52, 63, 82
Archaeological Specimens 13
Arms (Loose & Broken) 14 - 16
Astragal Glazing 17

B

Bamboo Furniture 18
Barometers 20, 21
Barograph 21
Basketwork 22
Beadwork 22
Beeswax 29, 36, 87
Bentwood 22, 23
Benzene 36
Benzole 58

Birch veneer 31, 101
Bisque 54
Bleaching 23 - 26
Blotches (to remove) 24
Bone 26
Bone Inlay 27
Books 24 - 30
Bookworm 29
Boulle (Andre Charles) 34
Boxwood 31, 20
Boxwood String Inlay 31
Brass 32, 34
Brass Inlay 32
British Museum Leather Dressing 29
Brobat 23
Bronze 33 - 34
Bronze Disease 34, 13
Brummer 61
Buhl 34

C

Candlewax (To Remove) 35
Canada Balsam 58
Canework 35
Canvas (to reline) 87
Carbon bisulphide 35
Carbon tetrachloride 49
Carborundum 11
Carpet beetles 49
Carpets 36
Cast iron 66
Castor oil 29, 71
Caustic Soda 89
Cedarwood oil 29
Celluloid 58
Chalk 50
Chalk Drawings 37
Champleve 58
Chandeliers 34
China 38 - 43
China paste 39

Chloride of lime — 26
Chlorine — 26
Chloroform — 35
Chronometers — **44**
Cigarette Burns — **45**, 25
Citric acid — 12
Clocks — **46**
Cloisonne — 58
Clothes Moths — **49**
Coins and Medals — **49**
Colour fastness (To test for) — 36
Copaiva Balsam — 87
Copper and Brass — **32**
Copper acetate — 33
Copper nitrate — 33
Cracks in Wood — **50**
Creases in paper — 30
Crocus powder — 11, 50
Cupping — 88
Cutlery — **52**

Dammar varnish — 87
Damp (Effects of, on drawers) — 56
Dents in Wood — **53**
Desk Tops (leather covered) — 71 - 72
Dolls — **53**
Domestos — 23
Dowelling — 14, 18
Drawers — **56**

Ebonised Furniture — **57**
Ebony — 34
Emery cloth — 11
Emery paper — 11
Enamel — **57**

Epoxy resin — 13, 32, 38, 48, 55, 66
Ethyl acetate — 86

Falling Apart — **58**
Feathering — 60
Fixative — 37
Flour Paste — 30
Flux — 85
Fossils — 13
Fox marks — 25, 29
Frames (Repairing) — 61
Frames (Reducing sizes of) — 61
Framing — **59**
French polishing — 92
Fuller's Earth — 36

Garnet paper — 11
Gelatine — 30
Gesso — **62**, 61, 86
Gilding — **62**
Gilding paste — 30
Glass — **62**
Glass cutting — 17, 18
Glass fibre — 50, 51
Glass paper — 11
Glass Stoppers (To remove) — 62, 63
Goddard's Furniture Cream — 92
Goddard's Silver Dip — 49
Gold — **64**, 49
Gold Leaf — **64**
Gold Size — 64
Grease Spots (to remove from paper) — 29
Ground glass — 63
Gum Arabic — 80
Gypsum — 62

H

Hammer (Ball peen)	85, 93
Hammer (Rubber headed)	58
Hammer (Soft)	58
Hazel Twigs	22
Heat Marks	**64**
Hexane	29
Hinges	**65**
Holes in paper	29
Horn	**66**
Hydrochloric acid	11, 25
Hydrogen Peroxide	26, 29, 38, 87

I

Ink Stains	24
Iron	**66**
Iron cement	66, 67
Ivory	67

J

Jade	**68**
Jadeite	68
Japanning	**68**
Jet	**68**
Jeweller's rouge	11, 62, 77, 98
Jewellery	**68**

L

Lace	69
Lacquer	70
Lanolin	29, 71
Lead	70
Leather	71, 27
Legs (Loose & broken)	72
Lemon juice	12, 32
Lighter fuel	20, 29
Limestone (To remove from metal)	49
Linseed oil	24, 65
Locks	**73**

M

Marble	**74**
Marquetry	**74**
Mastic Varnish	87
Mercury	20, 21
Metal polish	24
Methylated spirits	50
Milton	24
Mitre Guide	59
Mother of Pearl	**77**
Mounts	**77 - 80**
Mountants	**80**
Musical Boxes	**81**

N

Needlework	**82**
Nephrite	68
Nitric acid	11, 24, 49, 98

O

Oil of pine	36

Onyx 82
Ormolu 82
Osiers 22
Oval Mounts 80
Oxalic acid 11, 24, 33, 50

P

Packing 83
Packing of oil paintings 88
Paintings (care of) 88
Paintings (Siting of) 89
Paint (Removal of) 84
Papier Mache 84, 55
Paper (Repairing torn) 25
Paradichlorbenzene 49
Paraffin wax 13, 26
Parazone 23
Parquetry 85
Pastels 37
Patination of bronze 33
Penetrating oil 65
Perspex 63
Petrol 47
Pewter 85
Pictures (Oil) 86 - 89
Pine Furniture (To Strip) 89
Plaster Figures 91
Plaster of Paris 13, 40, 41, 91
Plasticene 38, 40
Plastic Padding 19
Plate (Sheffield) 92
Plique a jour 58
Polish 92
Polish (Removal of) 93
Polyurethane 19, 22
Polyvinyl acetate 12, 13, 66
Porcelain 25
Potato flour 82
Prints 94
Putty 38

R

Rentokil 49, 118
Resin 53, 87
Restoration Wax 62, 64, 82
Rivets 93
Rockers (To make & fit) 94
Rungs (Loose & broken) 94
Rushwork 95
Rust (Removal of) 117
Rust Spots on paper 25

S

Saddle Soap 29
Salt 33
Sash Cramps 52
Sawdust (as a cleanser) 36
Screws (Removal of) 96
Seagrass 96
Sealing wax 34
Shading 96
Sheerwax 28
Shellac 97
Shellac Stick 45, 51, 53, 100
Shoe dye 57
Shoe polish 29, 34, 35, 48
Silver 98
Silverfish 29
Size 86
Slats (Loose & broken) 98
Sodium Sesquicarbonate 34
Solder 99, 32,
Spelter 50, 99
Sperm oil 71

Spirits of salt   62
Splicing   16
Split Panels   **51**
Spots (To remove)   24
Stain   100
Stains (To remove)   24
Steel Wool   11, 24
Streaks (to remove)   24
Sulphuric acid   11
Sunshine (Bleaching effects of)   35, 96

T

Talc   11, 36, 69
Tambour (To replace)   **100**
Tankards (To repair)   85
Tea & Coffee Stains (Removal of
    from China)   38
Tears in paper   30
Tenon & Mortice (To remake)   15
Tooling leather   71
Tortoiseshell   **101**, 34
Treasure Wax   64
Tunbridge Ware   **101**
Turpentine   86

U

Upholstery   **102 - 113**

V

Vaseline   71
Veneer   **114**, 51, 58
Venice Turpentine   87
Vinegar   12, 24, 89

W

Warped Wood   115
Watches   **115**
Water Colours   25
Wax Dolls   55
Wax Figures   **116**
Wax polish   19
Wax Sticks   **116**, 33, 45, 48, 51
Weapons   **117**
Wet-or-Dry paper   12
White Spirit   36
White water marks   24
Whiting   11, 26
Wigs (Doll's)   55
Willow Twigs   22
Winton Picture Cleaner   86
Wire Brushes   33
Woodworm   **118**